lonely planet

Pocket
İSTANBUL

TOP SIGHTS • LOCAL LIFE • MADE EASY

D0348429

Virginia Maxwell

In This Book

QuickStart Guide

Your keys to understanding the city – we help you decide what to do and how to do it

Need to Know
Tips for a smooth trip

Neighbourhoods
What's where

Explore İstanbul

The best things to see and do, neighbourhood by neighbourhood

Top Sights
Make the most of your visit

Local Life
The insider's city

The Best of İstanbul

The city's highlights in handy lists to help you plan

Best Walks
See the city on foot

İstanbul's Best...
The best experiences

Survival Guide

Tips and tricks for a seamless, hassle-free city experience

Getting Around
Travel like a local

Essential Information
Including where to stay

Our selection of the city's best places to eat, drink and experience:

◎ **Sights**

✖ **Eating**

▣ **Drinking**

✪ **Entertainment**

🔒 **Shopping**

These symbols give you the vital information for each listing:

☎	Telephone Numbers	✦	Family-Friendly
⊙	Opening Hours	✿	Pet-Friendly
℗	Parking	🚌	Bus
⊖	Nonsmoking	⛴	Ferry
@	Internet Access	Ⓜ	Metro
🔊	Wi-Fi Access	Ⓢ	Subway
🔧	Vegetarian Selection	🚃	Tram
📖	English-Language Menu	🚆	Train

Find each listing quickly on maps for each neighbourhood:

Bar Hemingway

16 ▣ Map p233, B2

Legend has it that Hemi self, wielding a machine berate this timber-pan ered bar during showpiece is a en by Papa ar town. Dress s.com; Hôtel Rit ⊙6.30pm-2a

Lonely Planet's İstanbul

Lonely Planet Pocket Guides are designed to get you straight to the heart of the city.

Inside you'll find all the must-see sights, plus tips to make your visit to each one really memorable. We've split the city into easy-to-navigate neighbourhoods and provided clear maps so you'll find your way around with ease. Our expert authors have searched out the best of the city: walks, food, nightlife and shopping, to name a few. Because you want to explore, our 'Local Life' pages will take you to some of the most exciting areas to experience the real İstanbul.

And of course you'll find all the practical tips you need for a smooth trip: itineraries for short visits, how to get around, and how much to tip the guy who serves you a drink at the end of a long day's exploration.

It's your guarantee of a really great experience.

Our Promise

You can trust our travel information because Lonely Planet authors visit the places we write about, each and every edition. We never accept freebies for positive coverage, so you can rely on us to tell it like it is.

QuickStart Guide 7

Explore İstanbul 21

Worth a Trip:

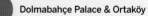

The Best of İstanbul 113

İstanbul's Best Walks

İstanbul's Best...

Survival Guide 133

QuickStart Guide

Welcome to İstanbul

In İstanbul, extraordinary experiences are found around every corner. Here, dervishes whirl, *müezzins* duel from minarets, and continents are crossed multiple times in a day. Home to millennia-old monuments and cutting-edge art galleries (sometimes in the same block), it's a destination where eating, drinking and dancing are local priorities, and where everyone is welcome to join the party.

Blue Mosque (p28)
GEORGE TSAFOS/GETTY IMAGES ©

İstanbul
Top Sights

Aya Sofya (p24)

History resonates when you visit this majestic basilica. Built in the 6th century AD, its remarkable features include a massive dome and a stunning collection of Byzantine mosaic portraits.

Topkapı Palace
(p42)

A series of mad, sad and downright bad sultans lived in this pavilion-style palace during the glory days of the Ottoman Empire. Reminders of their privileged lifestyles are everywhere to be seen.

The Bosphorus
(p108)

A ferry trip down the mighty Bosphorus strait showcases a passing parade of mosques, palaces and mansions on both the Asian and European shores.

Grand Bazaar (p56)

Sometimes described as the world's oldest and most evocative shopping mall, this colourful and chaotic covered market is the heart of İstanbul's Old City and one of its most atmospheric destinations.

Kariye Museum (Chora Church) (p74)

Great things come in small packages. This diminutive Byzantine church is made extraordinary by virtue of its interior, which is crammed with exquisite mosaics and frescoes.

İstanbul Archaeology Museums (p46)

An eclectic collection of antiquities, classical sculpture, Ottoman tile work and Byzantine artefacts is showcased at this museum complex next to Topkapı Palace.

Süleymaniye Mosque (p60)

Truly deserving of the tag 'living history', this imperial mosque atop the city's fourth hill is one of the few that has retained, restored and creatively reused its original outbuildings.

İstiklal Caddesi (p78)

A promenade down this pedestrianised 19th-century boulevard is the quintessential İstanbul experience, offering a colourful snapshot of local life.

İstanbul Modern (p80)

İstanbul has one of the most exciting contemporary art scenes in the world, and this gallery housed in a converted shipping warehouse on the Bosphorus is its pre-eminent venue.

Dolmabahçe Palace (p100)

This ornate palace on the Bosphorus shore – built as the Ottoman Empire's power waned, but making no concessions to this fact – gives a fascinating glimpse into the sultans' artificial lives and ostentatious taste.

MARK AVELLINO/GETTY IMAGES ©

TIM BARKER/GETTY IMAGES ©

Basilica Cistern (p30)

Both architectural tour de force and virtuosic engineering feat, this evocatively lit underground cistern is one of İstanbul's most mysterious and magnificent Byzantine monuments.

Blue Mosque (p28)

Beloved of tourists and locals alike, the most photogenic of İstanbul's imperial mosques is also one of the busiest places of worship in the city.

İstanbul
Local Life

Insider tips to help you find the real city

İstanbul's 14 million residents enjoy an exhilarating lifestyle that is crammed with culture, backdropped by history and underpinned by family and faith. Head to their neighbourhoods, mosques, shops and cafes to see what makes life here so special.

Between the Bazaars (p62)

▶ Local shopping
▶ Historic buildings

The winding streets linking the historic Grand and Spice Bazaars are crowded, colourful and cacophonous on every day of the week except Sunday. Locals have purchased provisions, outfitted themselves and stocked up on household goods of every possible description here for centuries, and most show no sign of moving their custom to the soulless shopping malls found in the suburbs. Celebrate this fact by punctuating your visit to the bazaars with some exploration here.

An Afternoon in Galata (p82)

▶ Fashion boutiques
▶ Designer homeware shops

Lying in the shadow of its medieval tower, the district of Galata melds its historic credentials (intact 19th-century streetscapes and churches, even older mosques and fortifications) with the city's best boutiques and an ever-growing avant-garde arts scene. An afternoon spent wandering, shopping and gallery-hopping will give you a seductive taste of bohemian life, İstanbullu style.

Weekend Wander in Ortaköy (p102)

▶ Snack and market stalls
▶ Bosphorus views

A former fishing village, Ortaköy makes the most of its magnificent Bosphorus location. Centred on a waterside square full of eateries and cafes, the suburb is home to one of the city's prettiest mosques and plays host to crowds of locals on weekends, who flock here to promenade, take ferry cruises, snack on local fast foods, browse the stalls of the Sunday handicrafts market and drink in the bars and cafes.

Spice Bazaar (p66)

Nargile (water pipe) cafe

Other great places and ways to experience the city like a local:

Manda Batmaz (p92)

Türkü Evleri (p96)

Fish Sandwiches (p68)

Hazzo Pulo Çay Bahçesi (p93)

Hocapaşa Sokak (p51)

Yeni Marmara (p38)

İstanbul Day Planner

Day One

With only one day, you'll need to get cracking! Head to Sultanahmet, where you can visit three of the city's top sights: the **Blue Mosque** (p28), **Aya Sofya** (p24) and the **Basilica Cistern** (p30). For lunch, sample the delights of Ottoman palace cuisine at nearby **Matbah** (p51) or **Cihannüma** (p51).

Walk up Yerebatan and Nuruosmaniye Caddesis to the **Grand Bazaar** (p56). Shop, explore, drink tea and practise your bargaining skills before following our local life itinerary (p62) down the winding shopping street linking the bazaar with the bustling transport hub of Eminönü. Afterwards, enjoy a bath and massage at one of the Old City's historic **hamams** (p124).

Cross the Galata Bridge to sample the nightlife in Beyoğlu. Kick off at a **rooftop bar** (p121), then move on to dinner at a traditional *meyhane* (tavern) such as **Asmalı Cavit** (p88) or a fireside kebap restaurant such as **Zübeyir Ocakbaşı** (p89). If you've still got energy, there are plenty of clubs and bars to keep you entertained into the early hours – current favourites are in the expat enclave of Cihangir, on the eastern edge of Taksim Sq, although **Babylon** (p95) in Asmalımescit is always a safe choice.

Day Two

Topkapı Palace (p42) is your first destination of the day. Spend at least three hours here, being sure not to miss the Harem and Marble Terrace, before walking down **Soğukçeşme Sokak** (p49) towards Eminönü. Stop for a simple lunch in **Hocapaşa Sokak** (p51) and a sweet treat at **Hafız Mustafa** (p51) along the way.

Take a tram and funicular to Taksim Sq, and walk down **İstiklal Caddesi** (p78), visiting cultural centres including **ARTER** (p79) and **SALT Beyoğlu** (p79) along the way. If you're interested in Orientalist art, make a detour to the **Pera Museum** (p87) in nearby Tepebaşı. Then follow our local life itinerary in **Galata** (p82) and watch the sun set over the Old City at **X Bar** (p94) or **Ca' d'Oro** (p89).

Enjoy dinner in the rapidly gentrifying enclave of Karaköy, close to the Galata Bridge – **Lokanta Maya** (p88) and **Karaköy Lokantası** (p89) are both great choices. After dinner, adjourn to **Karaköy Güllüoğlu** (p88) for a decadently rich plate of baklava, or follow the seductive scent of apple tobacco to the nargile (water pipe) cafes in **Tophane** (p92), where you are sure to encounter a colourful cast of locals.

Short on time?

We've arranged İstanbul's must-sees into these day-by-day itineraries to make sure you see the very best of the city in the time you have available.

Day Three

☼ Climb aboard the mid-morning Boğaz Gezileri ferry cruise heading down the **Bosphorus** (p108), marveling at the Ottoman-era mansions and palaces that line the Asian and European shores. Alight at Sarıyer, and take a bus or taxi to the pretty suburb of Emirgan, home to the impressive **Sakıp Sabancı Museum** (p110) and its glamorous restaurant, **MüzedeChanga** (p109).

☼ Continue on your journey back to town by bus, stopping to visit the majestic fortress of **Rumeli Hisarı** (p110), built by order of Mehmet the Conqueror. Have a rest at one of the *çay bahçesis* (tea gardens) next to the fortress or continue along the coast road to the ultrafashionable suburb of Bebek, where you can enjoy a coffee on the terrace of Starbucks, which offers a fantastic view over the water. From here continue on to **Lokum** (p107) in Kuruçeşme, where you can purchase exquisitely packaged Turkish delight to take home.

☾ Stay in the Bosphorus suburbs for dinner, eating sushi at **Zuma** (p106), Mod Med at **Vogue** (p106) or seafood mezes at **Sıdıka** (p105). Afterwards, dance the night away at one of the clubs on the **Golden Mile** (p106).

Day Four

☼ A visit to the impressive **İstanbul Modern** (p80) will give you a background briefing on contemporary Turkish visual art, as well as the chance to take in an ever-impressive program of travelling international shows. After viewing the exhibits, lunch in the museum's excellent **cafe-restaurant** (p90), which overlooks the Bosphorus, and check out the designer souvenirs at the gallery's gift shop.

☼ Take the Golden Horn (Haliç) ferry from Eminönü and alight at Ayvansaray, walking uphill alongside the historic city walls to reach the **Kariye Museum** (Chora Church; p75), a repository of exquisite Byzantine mosaics and frescoes.

☾ See the dervishes whirl at the **Hocapaşa Culture Centre** (p52) in Sirkeci before moving on to dinner on the rooftop of **Hamdi Restaurant** (p67) in Eminönü, a bustling place serving tasty kebaps and commanding amazing views over the city. If you've got energy to spare, consider enjoying a farewell drink or two in a bar in Asmalımescit, Beyoğlu's bohemian hub.

Need to Know

**For more information,
see Survival Guide (p133)**

Currency
Türk Lirası (Turkish Lira; ₺)

Language
Turkish

Visas
Not required for some European nationalities; most other nationalities can obtain a 90-day visa on arrival.

Money
ATMs are widely available. Credit cards are accepted at most shops, hotels and upmarket restaurants.

Mobile Phones
Most European and Australasian phones can be used here, but some North American phones can't. Check with your provider.

Time
Eastern European time (UTC/GMT plus two hours November to March; plus three hours April to October).

Plugs & Adaptors
Plugs have two round pins; electrical current is 230V. North American and Australasian visitors will require an adaptor.

Tipping
10% is usual in most restaurants. Round taxi fares up to the nearest lira.

① Before You Go

Your Daily Budget

Budget less than €60
▶ Dorm beds €13–20
▶ Kebap or pide dinner €9
▶ Beer at a neighbourhood bar €4

Midrange €60–200
▶ Double room from €70
▶ *Lokanta* lunch €12
▶ *Meyhane* dinner with wine €35

Top end more than €200
▶ Double room from €180
▶ Restaurant dinner with wine €45
▶ Cocktail in a rooftop bar €10

Useful Websites

Lonely Planet (www.lonelyplanet.com/istanbul) Destination information, traveller forum and more.

İstanbul Beat (www.istanbulbeatblog.com) Listings-based blog.

Cornucopia (www.cornucopia.net) Arts diary plus exhibitions listings and blogs.

Turkey Travel Planner (www.turkeytravelplanner.com) Useful travel information.

Advance Planning

▶ **Three months before** If you're travelling in spring, autumn or over Christmas, book your hotel as far in advance as possible.

▶ **Two months before** İstanbul's big-ticket festivals and concerts sell out fast; book tickets online at Biletix (www.biletix.com).

▶ **Two weeks before** Ask your hotel to make dinner reservations.

② Arriving in İstanbul

Two international airports service the city: Atatürk International Airport (IST, Atatürk Havalimanı; ☎212-463 3000; www.ataturkairport.com) and Sabiha Gökçen International Airport (SAW, Sabiha Gökçen Havalimanı; ☎216-588 8888; www.sgairport.com). At the time of research, only one international train service – the daily Bosfor/Balkan Ekspresi between İstanbul and Bucharest, Sofia and Belgrade – was operating in and out of İstanbul.

✈ From Atatürk International Airport

Destination	Best Transport
Sultanahmet	Metro & tram
Beyoğlu	Havataş Airport Bus
Bosphorus suburbs	Taxi

✈ From Sabiha Gökçen International Airport

Destination	Best Transport
Sultanahmet	Taxi
Beyoğlu	Havataş Airport Bus
Bosphorus suburbs	Taxi

✈ At the Airports

Atatürk International Airport There are ATMs, car-hire and accommodation booking desks, exchange bureaux, a 24-hour pharmacy, a left-luggage office and a PTT (post office) in the international arrivals hall. There is also a tourist information desk supplying maps, advice and brochures.

Sabiha Gökçen International Airport There are ATMs, car-hire and accommodation booking desks, exchange bureaux, a mini-market, a left-luggage office and a PTT in the international arrivals hall.

③ Getting Around

İstanbul has an extensive and generally efficient public transport system that will get even better with the new train lines and stations being delivered by the multi-billion-euro Marmaray (www.marmaray.com) project. When using public transport, you will save time, money and hassle by purchasing a rechargeable İstanbulkart transport card (see p137).

🚊 Tram

Services run from Bağcılar, in the city's west, to Kabataş, near Taksim Sq in Beyoğlu, stopping at stations including Zeytinburnu (to connect with the airport metro), Beyazıt-Kapalı Çarşı (Grand Bazaar), Sultanahmet, Karaköy and Eminönü en route.

⚓ Ferry

Boats travel between the Asian and European shores, up and down the Golden Horn (Haliç), and along and across the Bosphorus.

🚕 Taxi

Inexpensive and plentiful.

Ⓜ Metro

One line connects Aksaray with the airport. Another connects Şişhane, near Tünel Sq in Beyoğlu, with Taksim Sq and the commercial and residential districts to its northeast.

Funicular

These make the trip from the tramline up to İstiklal Caddesi in Beyoğlu easy. One connects Karaköy with Tünel; the other connects Kabataş with Taksim Sq.

Bus

The lines following the Bosphorus shoreline are of most interest to travellers. Be warned that trips are long and buses are crowded.

İstanbul Neighbourhoods

Worth a Trip
👁 Top Sights
Kariye Museum (Chora Church)

The Bosphorus

İstiklal Caddesi & Beyoğlu (p76)
Dominated by İstiklal, the city's most famous boulevard, this high-octane neighbourhood hosts the best eating, drinking and entertainment options.
👁 Top Sights
İstiklal Caddesi

İstanbul Modern

Grand Bazaar & the Bazaar District (p54)
A walk through this beguiling district features historic bazaars, chaotic local shopping streets and stunning imperial mosques.
👁 Top Sights
Grand Bazaar

Süleymaniye Mosque

Kariye Museum (Chora Church) 👁

İstiklal Caddesi 👁

Süleymaniye Mosque 👁

Grand Bazaar 👁

İstanbul Archaeology Museums 👁

Basilica Cistern 👁

Ay Sofy

Blue Mosque 👁

Dolmabahçe Palace

İstanbul Modern

Topkapı Palace

Topkapı Palace & Eminönü (p40)
A profusion of parks, pavilions, museums and scenic viewpoints gives this former stamping ground of the Ottoman sultans its unique allure.

☉ Top Sights
Topkapı Palace

İstanbul Archaeology Museums

Dolmabahçe Palace & Ortaköy (p98)
Opulent Ottoman palaces and ultrafashionable nightclubs can be found along this privileged and picturesque stretch of the Bosphorus shore.

☉ Top Sight
Dolmabahçe Palace

Aya Sofya & Sultanahmet (p22)
The famous Byzantine basilica is only one of many extraordinary museums and monuments in this ancient area.

☉ Top Sights
Aya Sofya

Blue Mosque

Basilica Cistern

Explore
İstanbul

Worth a Trip

Grand Bazaar (p56)
GARY YEOWELL/GETTY IMAGES ©

Explore

Aya Sofya & Sultanahmet

Many visitors to İstanbul never make it out of Sultanahmet. And while this is a shame, it's hardly surprising. After all, its mosques and museums – including the magnificent Aya Sofya – provide a time capsule of Byzantine and Ottoman history and culture unmatched anywhere in the world, and its impressive array of sights, shops, hotels and eateries are all within easy walking distance.

The Sights in a Day

☼ In İstanbul, all roads lead to the city's spiritual centre, Sultanahmet Park. Bookended by the grand edifices of Aya Sofya and the Blue Mosque, this unassuming garden is built over ruins of the Great Palace of Byzantium and is a good place to start your exploration of the neighbourhood. After visiting the **Blue Mosque** (p28), pop into the **Great Palace Mosaic Museum** (p33), browse the shops in the **Arasta Bazaar** (p29), then make your way to **Aya Sofya** (p24) and the **Aya Sofya Tombs** (p33).

☼ After lunch at **Cihannüma** (p51), wander through the **Hippodrome** (p35) and into the **Museum of Turkish & Islamic Arts** (p35), where you should visit the exhibits and enjoy a Turkish coffee at Müzenin Kahvesi in the courtyard. Afterwards, head to the **Basilica Cistern** (p30) and then relax over a sunset drink at the **Hotel Nomade Terrace Bar** (p36) or in the rear courtyard of the **Yeşil Ev** (p37).

☽ Sample some of the city's famous fish at **Ahırkapı Balıkçısı** (p35) or **Balıkçı Sabahattin** (p36) before winding down with a nargile (water pipe) at **Yeni Marmara** (p38), **Cafe Meşale** (p37) or **Derviş Aile Çay Bahçesi** (p37).

👁 Top Sights

Aya Sofya (p24)

Blue Mosque (p28)

Basilica Cistern (p30)

💜 Best of İstanbul

Museums

Museum of Turkish & Islamic Arts (p35)

Architecture

Aya Sofya (p24)

Blue Mosque (p28)

Basilica Cistern (p30)

Little Aya Sofya (p35)

Shopping

Cocoon (p38)

Jennifer's Hamam (p38)

Mehmet Çetinkaya Gallery (p38)

Tulu (p39)

Getting There

🚋 **Tram** Trams run between Bağcılar in the city's west and Kabataş near Taksim Sq in Beyoğlu. Alight at the Sultanahmet stop.

Top Sights
Aya Sofya

There are many important monuments in İstanbul, but this venerable structure – commissioned by Emperor Justinian and consecrated as a church in 537, converted to a mosque by Mehmet the Conqueror in 1453 and declared a museum by Atatürk in 1934 – surpasses the rest due to its rich history, religious importance and extraordinary beauty. Known as Hagia Sophia in Greek, Sancta Sophia in Latin and the Church of the Divine Wisdom in English, it is commonly acknowledged as one of the world's greatest buildings.

Hagia Sophia

⊙ Map p32, D1

www.ayasofyamuzesi. gov.tr

Aya Sofya Meydanı 1

adult/under 12yr ₺25/ free

⊙9am-6pm Tue-Sun

🚇Sultanahmet

Don't Miss

Imperial Door

The main entrance into the nave is crowned with a mosaic of Christ as Pantocrator (Ruler of All). Christ holds a book that carries the inscription 'Peace be With You. I am the Light of the World' and is flanked by the Virgin Mary and the Archangel Gabriel. At his feet an emperor (probably Leo VI) prostrates himself.

Nave

Made 'transparent' by its profusion of windows and columned arcades, Aya Sofya's nave is as visually arresting as it is enormous. The chandeliers hanging low above the floor are Ottoman additions, as are the 19th-century medallions inscribed with gilt Arabic letters and the elevated kiosk where the sultan worshipped.

Apse

The 9th-century mosaic of the Virgin and Christ Child in the apse is the focal point of the nave. A *mimber* (pulpit) and *mihrab* (prayer niche indicating the direction of Mecca) were added by the Ottomans.

Dome

The famous dome measures 30m in diameter and 56m in height. It is supported by 40 massive ribs resting on four huge pillars concealed in the interior walls. On its completion, the Byzantine historian Procopius described it as being 'hung from heaven on a golden chain'.

Seraphs

The four huge winged angels at the base of the dome were originally mosaic, but two (on the western side) were recreated as frescoes after being damaged in the 13th century. All four faces

---

☑ **Top Tips**

▶ The museum is at its busiest first thing in the morning and in the mid-afternoon, when tour groups descend en masse. Visit during lunchtime or late in the day to avoid the crowds and long ticket queue.

▶ Bypass the ticket queue by prepurchasing a Museum Pass İstanbul (p140).

▶ Bring binoculars if you want to properly view the mosaic portraits in the apse and under the dome.

▶ Visit the nave first (entering through the Imperial Door), followed by the upstairs galleries.

▶ Hours vary; see the website for details.

✕ **Take a Break**

Retreat to the tranquil courtyard at nearby Yeşil Ev (p37) hotel to escape the crowds and enjoy a drink or light lunch.

The Cihannüma (p51) restaurant in the And Hotel offers tasty food and spectacular views.

were covered by metallic discs during the Ottoman period, and are slowly being restored. One was unveiled in 2009.

Saints Mosaics

When in the nave, look up towards the northeast (to your left if you are facing the apse), and you will see three mosaics at the base of the northern tympanum (semicircle) beneath the dome. These are 9th-century portraits of St Ignatius the Younger, St John Chrysostom and St Ignatius Theodorus of Antioch. Next to them (but only visible from the upstairs north gallery) is a mosaic portrait of Emperor Alexandros.

Weeping Column

Legend has it that this column in the northeast aisle was blessed by St Gregory the Miracle Worker and that putting one's finger into its hole can lead to ailments being healed if the finger emerges moist.

Upstairs Galleries

To access the galleries, walk up the switchback ramp at the northern end of the inner narthex. When you reach the top, you'll find a large circle of green marble marking the spot where the throne of the empress once stood. The view over the main space towards the apse from this vantage point is quite spectacular.

Aya Sofya – Ground Floor & Upstairs Galleries

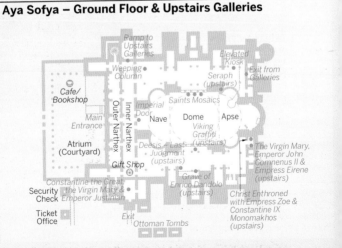

Deesis (Last Judgment)

The remnants of this magnificent 13th-century mosaic are in the upstairs south gallery. It depicts Christ with the Virgin Mary on his left and John the Baptist on his right.

Grave of Enrico Dandolo

Dandolo, who was Doge of Venice, led the soldiers of the Fourth Crusade who conquered Constantinople in 1204. He died in the city the following year, and was buried in Aya Sofya's upper gallery. A 19th-century marker indicates the probable location of his grave.

Christ Enthroned with Empress Zoe & Constantine IX Monomakhos

This mosaic portrait in the upper gallery depicts Zoe (r 1042), one of only three Byzantine women to rule as empress in their own right.

The Virgin Mary, Emperor John Comnenus II & Empress Eirene

Another wonderful mosaic, this time featuring 'John the Good' on the Virgin's left and his wife, who was known for her charitable works, on the Virgin's right. Their son Alexius, who died soon after the portrait was made, is depicted next to Eirene.

Viking Graffiti

Graffiti dating from the 9th century is carved into a marble banister in the upstairs south balcony. It is thought to have been the work of a mercenary called Halvdan.

The mosque's altar

Constantine the Great, the Virgin Mary & Emperor Justinian

As you exit the building, don't miss this 10th-century mosaic showing Constantine (right) offering the Virgin Mary the city of Constantinople; Justinian (left) is offering her Hagia Sophia.

Ottoman Tombs

The beautifully decorated tombs (p33) of five Ottoman sultans and their families are located in Aya Sofya's southern corner and accessed via Kabasakal Caddesi. One of these occupies the church's original Baptistry.

Top Sights
Blue Mosque

İstanbul's most photogenic building was the grand project of Sultan Ahmet I (r 1603–17), whose *türbe* (tomb) is located on the northern side of the site facing Sultanahmet Park and Aya Sofya. The mosque's wonderfully curvaceous exterior features a huge courtyard, a cascade of domes and six slender minarets (more than any other Ottoman mosque). Inside, thousands of blue İznik tiles adorn the walls and give the building its unofficial but commonly used name.

Sultan Ahmet Camii

⊙ Map p32, C3

Hippodrome

⊙ 9am-12.15pm, 2-4.30pm & 5.30-6.30pm Sat-Thu, 9-11.15am, 2.30-4.30pm & 5.30-6.30pm Fri

🚊 Sultanahmet

Don't Miss

The Ceremonial Entrance

The mosque is best approached via the Hippodrome. When entering the courtyard, you'll be able to appreciate the perfect proportions of the building and see how a progression of domes draws worshippers' eyes from ground level (ie earth) to the dome and minarets (ie heaven).

Prayer Hall

The 260 stained-glass windows and mass of İznik tiles immediately attract attention, and the dome and semidomes are painted with graceful arabesques. Notable structures include an elevated kiosk covered with marble latticework; a *mihrab* featuring a piece of the sacred Black Stone from the Kaaba in Mecca; a high *mahfil* (chair) from which the imam gives the sermon on Fridays; and a beautifully carved white marble *mimber*.

The Mosque Complex

Imperial mosques usually incorporated public-service institutions such as hospitals, soup kitchens and hamams. Here, a large *medrese* (Islamic school of higher studies; closed to the public) and *arasta* (row of shops by a mosque; now the **Arasta Bazaar**) remain. The rent from shops in the *arasta* has always supported the upkeep of the mosque; the best shopping in Sultanahmet is found in and around this historic arcade.

Tomb of Sultan Ahmet I

Ahmet died one year after his mosque was constructed, aged only 27. Buried with him are his wife, Kösem, who was strangled to death in the Topkapı Harem, and his sons, Sultan Osman II, Sultan Murat IV and Prince Beyazıt (strangled by order of Murat). Like the mosque, the tomb features fine İznik tiles.

☑ Top Tips

▶ Only worshippers are admitted through the main eastern door; tourists must use the northern door (follow the signs).

▶ Women should bring a shawl to cover head and shoulders; those without one will be loaned a headscarf.

▶ Shoes must be removed before entering the prayer hall; it's best to carry them with you in a plastic bag (provided) rather than leaving them on the shelves.

✗ Take a Break

The leafy Derviş Aile Çay Bahçesi (p37) opposite the mosque is a good spot for tea, fresh juice and people-watching.

For simple but tasty Anatolian dishes in pleasant modern surrounds, head to nearby Cooking Alaturka (p36).

Top Sights
Basilica Cistern

Commissioned by Emperor Justinian, this subterranean structure was built in 532 beneath the Stoa Basilica, a great square that occupied Byzantium's First Hill. The largest surviving Byzantine cistern in İstanbul, it features a forest of 336 marble and granite columns, many of which were salvaged from ruined classical temples and have fine carved capitals. The cistern's symmetry and sheer grandeur of conception are quite breathtaking, making it a favourite location for big-budget films (remember *From Russia with Love*?).

Yerebatan Sarnıçı

⦿ Map p32, C1

www.yerebatan.com

Yerebatan Caddesi 13

admission ₺10

🕘9am-6.30pm

🚊Sultanahmet

Don't Miss

Columns

The cistern's columns are all 9m high; most have Ionic and Corinthian capitals. Arranged in 12 rows, they include one engraved with shapes that are often described as peacock's eyes, or tears. Some historians assert that these tears were carved to pay tribute to the hundreds of slaves who died during the construction of the cistern.

Medusa Heads

Two columns feature striking bases carved with the head of Medusa. One is upside down, the other on its side. When the building functioned as a cistern, both would have lain beneath the surface of the water. Now revealed, they provide the building with an element of mystery.

The Fish

The cistern was built to store water for the Great Palace of Byzantium, a sprawling complex occupying the area between the Hippodrome and the Sea of Marmara. After the Conquest, it supplied water to irrigate the gardens of Topkapı Palace. Decommissioned in the 19th century, its shallow water is now home to ghostly patrols of carp and goldfish that can be seen from the cistern's elevated wooden walkways.

☑ Top Tips

▸ The cistern is a blissfully cool retreat on hot summer days – visit in the afternoon, when the city's heat can be particularly oppressive.

▸ Watch young children carefully, as the walkways over the water don't have much of a safety barrier.

✗ Take a Break

Hafız Mustafa (p36) is a great spot to enjoy a glass of tea and sweet treats such as baklava and fırın sutlaç (rice pudding).

For a cheap and tasty lunch, head to Sefa Restaurant (p52), a popular lokanta (eatery serving ready-made Turkish food) – try to arrive at the start of service, as dishes tend to sell out quickly.

For reviews see

◆ Top Sights		p24
● Sights		p33
✕ Eating		p35
❶ Drinking		p36
❶ Shopping		p38

200 m
0.1 miles

Aya Sofya Tombs

Sights

Aya Sofya Tombs   TOMBS

1 Map p32, D2

Part of the Aya Sofya complex but entered via Kabasakal Caddesi, these tombs are the final resting places of five sultans – Mehmed III, Selim II, Murad III, İbrahim I and Mustafa I – most of whom are buried with members of their families. The ornate interior decoration in the tombs features the very best Ottoman tilework, calligraphy and decorative paintwork. (Aya Sofya Müzesi Padişah Türbeleri; Kabasakal Caddesi; admission free; ⊘9am-5pm; ⊠Sultanahmet)

Great Palace Mosaic Museum   MUSEUM

2 Map p32, C3

When archaeologists from the University of Ankara and the University of St Andrews (Scotland) excavated around the Arasta Bazaar at the rear of the Blue Mosque in the mid-1950s, they uncovered a stunning mosaic pavement featuring hunting and mythological scenes. Dating from early Byzantine times, it was restored between 1983 and 1997 and is now preserved in this museum. (Torun Sokak; admission ₺8; ⊘9am-6.30pm Tue-Sun Apr-Oct, to 4.30pm Nov-Mar; ⊠Sultanahmet)

Understand
Byzantium

Known for its charismatic emperors, powerful armies, refined culture and convoluted politics, Byzantium's legacy resonates to this day.

The Eastern Roman Empire

Legend tells us that the city of Byzantium was founded in 667 BC by a group of colonists from Megara, northwest of Athens, led by Byzas, the son of Megara's king. An alliance was eventually formed with the Romans, and the city was officially incorporated into their empire in AD 79. In the late 3rd century, Emperor Diocletian (r 284–305) split the empire into eastern and western administrative units. His actions resulted in a civil war in which a rival, Constantine I, triumphed. Constantine made Byzantium his capital in 330, naming it 'New Rome'.

The new capital soon came to be known as Constantinople. Constantine died in 337, but the city continued to grow under the rule of emperors including Theodosius I ('the Great'; r 379–95), Theodosius II (r 408–50) and Justinian (r 527–65). The eastern and western empires had been politically separated after the death of Theodosius I, but the final tie with Rome wasn't severed until 620, when Heraclius I (r 610–41) changed the official language of the eastern empire from Latin to Greek, inaugurating what we now refer to as the 'Byzantine Empire'.

The Byzantine Empire

For the next eight centuries the empire asserted its independence from Rome by adopting Orthodox Christianity. Ruled by a series of family dynasties, it was the most powerful economic, cultural and military force in Europe until the Seljuk Turks acquired much of its territory in Asia Minor in 1071.

In 1204 Constantinople fell to Latin soldiers of the Fourth Crusade. The powerful Byzantine families went into exile in Nicaea and Epirus, and the empire was split between Greek and Latin factions. Despite being reclaimed by the Nicaean emperor Michael VIII Palaiologos in 1261, it was plagued by a series of civil wars and finally fell to the Ottomans in 1453, when Mehmet II (Fatih, or Conqueror) took Constantinople. The last Byzantine emperor, Constantine XI Palaiologos, died defending the walls from Mehmet's onslaught.

Hippodrome PARK

3 ⊙ Map p32, B2

The Byzantines loved nothing more than an afternoon at the chariot races, and this rectangular arena was their venue of choice. Originally, it consisted of two levels of galleries, the racetrack, starting boxes and the semicircular end known as the Sphendone. At its centre is the granite Obelisk of Theodosius, brought from Egypt by the emperor in AD 390. (Atmeydanı; ☒Sultanahmet)

Museum of Turkish & Islamic Arts MUSEUM

4 ⊙ Map p32, B2

This Ottoman palace was built in 1524 for İbrahim Paşa, childhood friend, brother-in-law and grand vizier of Süleyman the Magnificent. It's now home to an outstanding collection of artefacts, including an assortment of antique carpets generally held to be the best in the world. While here, be sure to enjoy an expertly prepared Turkish coffee at **Müzenin Kahvesi** in the courtyard. (Türk ve Islam Eserleri Müzesi; www.tiem.gov.tr; Atmeydanı Caddesi 46; admission ₺10; ⏰9am-6.30pm Tue-Sun Apr-Oct, to 4.30pm Nov-Mar; ☒Sultanahmet)

Little Aya Sofya MOSQUE

5 ⊙ Map p32, A4

Justinian and his wife Theodora built this little church sometime between 527 and 536, just before Justinian built Aya Sofya. You can still see their

monogram worked into some of the frilly white capitals. Recently restored, the building is one of the most beautiful Byzantine structures in the city. It now functions as a mosque. (Küçük Aya Sofya Camii, SS Sergius & Bacchus Church; Küçük Ayasofya Caddesi, Küçük Ayasofya; admission free; ☒Sultanahmet or Çemberlitaş)

Eating

Ahırkapı Balıkçısı SEAFOOD $$

6 ✗ Map p32, D4

For years we've been promising locals not to list this neighbourhood fish restaurant in our book. We sympathised with their desire to retain the place's low profile, particularly as it's tiny and relatively cheap. However, the food here is so good and the eating alternatives in this area so bad that we've finally decided to share the secret. Book ahead. (☏212-518 4988; Keresteci

Hakkı Sokak 46, Cankurtaran; mezes ₺5-25, fish ₺15-70; ⏱4-11pm; 🚇Sultanahmet)

Balıkçı Sabahattin   SEAFOOD $$$

7 🍴 Map p32, D3

The limos outside Balıkçı Sabahattin pay testament to its enduring popularity with the city's establishment, who join cashed-up tourists in enjoying its limited menu of meze and fish. The food is excellent, though the service is often harried. You'll dine in a wooden Ottoman house or under a leafy canopy in the garden. (☎212-458 1824; www.balikcisabahattin.com; Seyit Hasan Koyu Sokak 1, Cankurtaran; mezes ₺10-30, fish ₺30-60; ⏱noon-midnight; 🚇Sultanahmet)

Cooking Alaturka   TURKISH $$

8 🍴 Map p32, D3

Dutch-born owner-chef Eveline Zoutendijk and her Turkish colleague Fehzi Yıldırım serve a set four-course menu of simple Anatolian dishes at this tranquil restaurant near the Blue Mosque. The menu makes the most of fresh seasonal produce, and can be tailored to suit vegetarians or those with food allergies (call ahead). No children under six at dinner and no credit cards. (☎212-458 5919; www.cookingalaturka.com; Akbıyık Caddesi 72a, Cankurtaran; set lunch or dinner ₺50; ⏱lunch Mon-Sat & dinner by reservation Mon-Sat; 🚇Sultanahmet)

Hafız Mustafa   SWEETS $

9 🍴 Map p32, C1

Located in the Kıraathanesi Foundation of Turkish Literature, this branch of one of the city's most popular şekerlemelerilar (sweets shops) is a great place for a mid-morning or mid-afternoon pit stop. (www.hafizmustafa.com; Divan Yolu Caddesi 14; börek ₺5, baklava ₺6-7.50, puddings ₺6; 🚇Sultanahmet)

Teras Restaurant   TURKISH $$$

10 🍴 Map p32, E3

The terrace restaurant at this upmarket hotel offers good food, killer views of the Blue Mosque, Aya Sofya and Sea of Marmara, an excellent (and affordable) wine list and very comfortable seating – a compelling combination indeed. Added extras come courtesy of a kids menu (₺12 to ₺14) and decent coffee. (☎212-455 4455; www.armadahotel.com.tr/pg_en/terrace.asp; Hotel Armada, Ahırkapı Sokak 24, Cankurtaran; mezes ₺7-15, mains ₺22-39; ⏱lunch & dinner; 🚇Sultanahmet)

Drinking

Hotel Nomade Terrace Bar   BAR

11 🍷 Map p32, B1

The intimate terrace of this boutique hotel overlooks Aya Sofya and the Blue Mosque. Settle down in a comfortable chair to enjoy a glass of wine, beer or freshly squeezed fruit juice. The only music that will disturb

Museum of Turkish & Islamic Arts (p35)

your evening's reverie is the Old City's signature sound of the call to prayer. (www.hotelnomade.com; Ticarethane Sokak 15, Alemdar; ⏰noon-11pm; 🚊Sultanahmet)

Yeşil Ev
BAR, CAFE

12 🚊 Map p32, D2

The elegant rear courtyard of this Ottoman-style hotel is a true oasis for those wanting to enjoy a quiet drink. In spring, flowers and blossoms fill every corner; in summer the fountain and trees keep the temperature down. You can order a sandwich, salad or cheese platter if you're peckish. (Kabasakal Caddesi 5; ⏰noon-10.30pm; 🚊Sultanahmet)

Derviş Aile Çay Bahçesi
TEA GARDEN

13 🚊 Map p32, C2

Superbly located directly opposite the Blue Mosque, the Derviş beckons patrons with its comfortable cane chairs and shady trees. Efficient service, reasonable prices and peerless people-watching opportunities make it a great place for a leisurely tea, nargile and game of backgammon. (Mimar Mehmet Ağa Caddesi; ⏰9am-11pm Apr-Oct; 🚊Sultanahmet)

Cafe Meşale
NARGILE CAFE

14 🚊 Map p32, C3

Located in a sunken courtyard behind the Blue Mosque, Meşale is a tourist trap par excellence but still has loads of charm. Generations of backpackers have joined locals in claiming one of its cushioned benches and enjoying a tea and nargile. There's sporadic live Turkish music and a bustling vibe in the evening. (Arasta Bazaar, Utangaç Sokak; ⊘24hr; 🚇Sultanahmet)

Türk Ocağı Kültür ve Sanat Merkezi İktisadi İşletmesi Çay Bahçesi TEA GARDEN

15 Map p32, A1

Tucked into the rear right-hand corner of a shady courtyard filled with Ottoman tombs, this enormously popular tea garden is a perfect place to escape the crowds and relax over a tea and nargile. (cnr Divan Yolu & Bab-ı Ali Caddesis, Çemberlitaş; ⊘8am-midnight; 🚇Çemberlitaş)

Shopping

Cocoon CARPETS, TEXTILES

16 Map p32, C4

There are so many rug and textile shops in İstanbul that choosing individual shops to recommend is incredibly difficult. We had no problem whatsoever in singling this one out, though. Felt hats, antique costumes and textiles from Central Asia are artfully displayed in four branches – two on Küçük Ayasofya Caddesi, one in the Arasta Bazaar and another in the Grand Bazaar. (www.cocoontr.com; Küçük Aya Sofya Caddesi 13; ⊘8.30am-7.30pm; 🚇Sultanahmet)

Local Life
Yeni Marmara

A neighbourhood tea house, **Yeni Marmara** (Map p32, B4; Çayıroğlu Sokak, Küçük Ayasofya; ⊘10am-1am; 🚇Sultanahmet) is frequented by backgammon-playing regulars who slurp tea, trade local gossip and puff on nargiles (water pipes). In winter a wood stove keeps the place cosy; in summer patrons sit on the rear terrace, which overlooks the Sea of Marmara.

Jennifer's Hamam BATHWARE

17 Map p32, C3

Owned by Canadian Jennifer Gaudet, the two Arasta Bazaar branches of this shop stock top-quality hamam items including towels, robes and *peştemals* (bath wraps) produced on old-style hand-shuttled looms. It also sells natural soaps and *kese* (coarse cloth mittens used for exfoliation). (www.jennifershamam.com; 43 & 135 Arasta Bazaar; ⊘9am-10.30pm Apr-Sep, 9am-7.30pm Oct-Mar; 🚇Sultanahmet)

Mehmet Çetinkaya Gallery CARPETS, TEXTILES

18 Map p32, C4

Mehmet Çetinkaya is known as one of the country's foremost experts on antique oriental carpets and kilims (pileless woven rugs). His flagship store-cum-gallery stocks items that have artistic and ethnographic significance, and is full of treasures. There's a second shop selling rugs, textiles and objects in the Arasta Bazaar. (www.cetinkayagallery.com; Tavukhane Sokak 7; ◷9.30am-7.30pm; 🚇Sultanahmet)

Khaftan   ART, ANTIQUES

19 🔒 Map p32, B3

Owner Adnan Cakariz sells antique Kütahya and İznik ceramics to collectors and museums here and overseas, so you can be sure that the pieces he sells in his own establishment are top-notch. Gleaming Russian icons, delicate calligraphy (old and new), ceramics, Karagöz puppets and contemporary paintings are all on show in this gorgeous shop. (www.khaftan.com; Nakilbent Sokak 33; ◷9am-8pm; 🚇Sultanahmet)

Tulu   HOMEWARES

20 🔒 Map p32, B3

One of the new breed of contemporary homeware stores taking İstanbul by storm, Tulu is owned by American Elizabeth Hewitt, a textile collector and designer who produces a stylish range of cushions, bedding and accessories inspired by textiles from Central Asia. These are sold alongside an array of furniture, textiles and objects sourced in countries including Uzbekistan, India, Japan and Indonesia. (www.tulutextiles.com; Üçler Sokak 7; 🚇Sultanahmet)

Yilmaz Ipekçilik   TEXTILES

21 🔒 Map p32, E3

Well-priced hand-loomed silk textiles made in Antakya are on sale in this slightly out of the way shop. Family-run, the business has been operating since 1950 and specialises in producing good-quality scarves, shawls and *peştemals*. (www.yilmazipekcilik.com/en; İshakpaşa Caddesi 36, Cankurtaran; ◷9am-9pm Mon-Sat, to 7pm in winter; 🚇Sultanahmet)

Explore

Topkapı Palace & Eminönü

The leafy parks and gardens in and around this opulent Ottoman palace stand in stark contrast to the crowded shopping streets clustered around the Eminönü ferry docks, but both areas are full of life and well worth a visit. Topkapı is perennially packed with tourists and Eminönü with locals; between them lies Gülhane Park, a tranquil retreat popular with both groups.

The Sights in a Day

☼ **Topkapı Palace** (p42) is one of Turkey's most compelling cultural attractions, so you'll need a full half-day to do it justice; start early to make the most of your time. After exploring all four courtyards of this historically significant landmark, make sure you detour into **Soğukçeşme Sokak** (p49) to admire one of the city's prettiest streetscapes.

☼ After sampling the Ottoman palace cuisine recreated by a series of chef-historians at **Matbah** (p51), continue your day's Ottoman theme at the **İstanbul Archaeology Museums** (p46), home to the palace collections acquired by the sultans. Afterwards, enjoy the tea and panoramic view on offer at **Set Üstü Çay Bahçesi** (p52) in **Gülhane Park** (p49), then head to Eminönü to stock up on *lokum* (Turkish delight) at one of the city's oldest shops, **Ali Muhiddin Hacı Bekir** (p53).

☾ Watch dervishes whirl at the **Hocapaşa Culture Center** (p52), enjoy dinner at **Paşazade** (p51) and – if you've still got energy and an appetite – head for a sweet finale at **Hafız Mustafa** (p52).

◉ Top Sights

Topkapı Palace (p42)

İstanbul Archaeology Museums (p46)

🖤 Best of İstanbul

Eating

Cihannüma (p51)

Matbah (p51)

Hafız Mustafa (p51)

Shopping

Ali Muhiddin Hacı Bekir (p53)

Getting There

🚋 **Tram** Trams run between Bağcılar in the city's west and Kabataş near Taksim Sq in Beyoğlu, stopping at Sultanahmet and Eminönü en route.

Top Sights
Topkapı Palace

Topkapı is the subject of more colourful stories than most of the world's museums put together. Libidinous sultans, ambitious courtiers, beautiful concubines and scheming eunuchs lived and worked here between the 15th and 19th centuries when the palace was the seat of the Ottoman sultanate. Visiting its opulent pavilions, landscaped courtyards, jewel-filled Treasury and sprawling Harem gives a fascinating glimpse into the lives of the sultans and their families, as well as offering an insight into the history and customs of a once mighty empire.

Topkapı Sarayı

Map p48, D3

www.topkapisarayi.gov.tr

Babıhümayun Caddesi

palace ₺25, Harem ₺15

9am-6pm Wed-Mon mid-Apr–Sep, to 4pm Oct–mid-Apr

Sultanahmet

Don't Miss

First Court

Before you enter the Imperial Gate (Bab-ı Hümayun), pause to view the gorgeous rococo-style **Fountain of Sultan Ahmet III** in the middle of the cobbled roundabout. Passing through the gate, you will enter the Court of the Janissaries, also known as the First Court. On your left is the Byzantine church of Hagia Eirene, more commonly known as Aya İrini (p49).

Second Court

The second of the palace's huge courtyards is home to audience pavilions, barracks, kitchens and sleeping quarters. Be sure to visit the Outer Treasury, where an impressive collection of Ottoman and European armoury is displayed.

Imperial Council Chamber

This ornate chamber on the left (west) side of the Second Court is where the Imperial Divân (Council) made laws, where citizens presented petitions and where foreign dignitaries were presented to the court. The sultan eavesdropped on proceedings through the gold grille high in the wall.

Harem

This complex on the western side of the Second Court was the private quarters of the sultans and their families. It features many opulently decorated bedchambers, reception rooms, hamams and courtyards. Highlights include the Salon of the Valide, Imperial Hall, Privy Chamber of Murat III, Privy Chamber of Ahmet III and Twin Kiosk/Apartments of the Crown Prince.

Third Court

The Third Court is entered through the impressive **Gate of Felicity**, a rococo-style structure

☑ Top Tips

▶ If you're visiting the Harem – and we recommend you do – you'll need to buy a separate ticket from the dedicated ticket office next to its entrance. See the website for Harem hours.

▶ Be sure to admire the spectacular views from the terrace behind the Imperial Treasury and from the İftariye Kameriyesi in the Fourth Court.

▶ Topkapı Palace can be accessed from both the Gülhane and Sultanahmet tram stops, but note that it's a steep uphill walk from Gülhane.

✗ Take a Break

There are good views from many of the terrace tables in the palace's Konyalı Restaurant, which is located in the Fourth Court, but the quality of food and level of service leave a lot to be desired.

To enjoy an Ottoman feast fit for a sultan, head to Matbah (p51), just outside the palace walls.

that was used for state ceremonies including the sultan's accession and funeral. Behind it was the sultan's private domain, staffed and guarded by eunuchs.

Audience Chamber
Important officials and foreign ambassadors were brought to this pavilion for imperial audiences. The sultan, seated on cushions embroidered with hundreds of seed pearls, inspected the ambassador's gifts and offerings as they were passed through the small doorway on the left.

Library of Ahmet III
Directly behind the Audience Chamber is this pretty library, built in 1719 for Sultan Ahmet III. Light-filled, it has comfortable reading areas and stunning inlaid woodwork.

Costume Collection
On the eastern edge of the Third Court is the Dormitory of the Expeditionary Force, which now houses a rich collection of imperial robes, kaftans and uniforms worked in silver and gold thread. Also here is a fascinating collection of talismanic shirts, which were believed to protect the wearer from enemies and misfortunes.

Sacred Safekeeping Rooms
Sumptuously decorated with İznik tiles, these rooms are a repository for many sacred relics. When the sultans lived here, the rooms were only opened once a year on the 15th day of the holy month of Ramazan.

Dormitory of the Privy Chamber
This dormitory next to the Sacred Safekeeping Rooms now houses portraits of 36 sultans. It includes a copy of Gentile Bellini's portrait of Mehmet the Conqueror and a wonderful painting of the *Enthronment Ceremony of Sultan Selim III* (1789) by court painter Kostantin Kapidagi.

Imperial Treasury
The Treasury's most famous exhibit is the Topkapı Dagger, which features three enormous emeralds on its hilt. Also here is the Kaşıkçı (Spoonmaker's) Diamond, a teardrop-shaped 86-carat rock surrounded by dozens of smaller stones. First worn by Mehmet IV at his accession to the throne in 1648, it's one of the largest diamonds in the world.

Marble Terrace
This gorgeous terrace in the Fourth Court is home to the Baghdad and Revan Kiosks, wonderful examples of classical palace architecture built in 1636 and 1639 respectively. The smaller Sünnet Odası (Circumcision Room) dates from 1640 and has outer walls covered with particularly beautiful İznik tiles.

İftariye Kameriyesi
During Ramazan, the sultans would enjoy their *iftar* (breaking of the fast) under this gilded canopy overlooking the Bosphorus and Golden Horn (Haliç). These days, it's a popular location for happy snaps.

Topkapı Palace

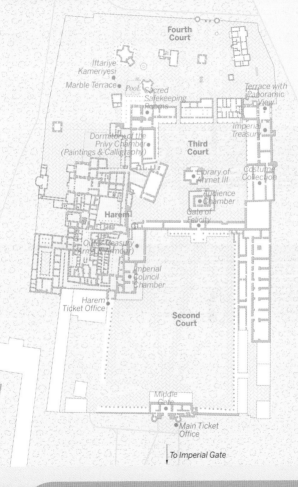

Fourth Court

İftariye Kameriyesi
Marble Terrace
Pool
Sacred Safekeeping Rooms
Terrace with Panoramic View
Imperial Treasury
Dormitory of the Privy Chamber (Paintings & Calligraphy)
Third Court
Library of Ahmet III
Costume Collection
Audience Chamber
Gate of Felicity
Harem
Outer Treasury (Arms & Armour)
Imperial Council Chamber
Harem Ticket Office
Second Court
Middle Gate
Main Ticket Office
To Imperial Gate

Top Sights
İstanbul Archaeology Museums

This superb museum complex houses archaeological and artistic treasures from the Imperial collections. Housed in three buildings that were once part of Topkapı Palace, its exhibits include ancient artefacts, classical statuary and objects showcasing Anatolian history. Though there are many highlights, history buffs will find the *İstanbul Through the Ages* exhibition, which focuses on the city's Byzantine past, particularly satisfying, and admirers of classical art will be blown away by the carved Alexander and Mourning Women Sarcophagi.

Map p48, C3

www.istanbularkeoloji.gov.tr

Osman Hamdi Bey Yokuşu, Gülhane

admission ₺10

⊙9am-6pm Tue-Sun mid-Apr–Sep, till 4pm Oct–mid-Apr

🚇Gülhane

Don't Miss

Archaeology Museum

This imposing neoclassical building is the heart of the museum complex. It houses an extensive collection of classical statuary and sarcophagi, including the extraordinary **Alexander Sarcophagus**, carved out of Pentelic marble and dating from the last quarter of the 4th century BC.

The Columned Sarcophagi of Anatolia

Amazingly detailed sarcophagi dating from between 140 and 270 AD feature in this exhibit. Many look like tiny temples or residential buildings; don't miss the **Sidamara Sarcophagus** from Konya.

İstanbul Through the Ages

Tracing the city's history using objects and interpretive panels, this exhibit has two sections: a dusty but undeniably fascinating floor above the Statuary Galleries filled with Archaic, Hellenistic, Roman and Ottoman artefacts; and an impressive downstairs gallery showcasing Byzantine objects.

Museum of the Ancient Orient

To your immediate left as you enter the complex, this 1883 building showcases a collection of pre-Islamic items collected from the expanse of the Ottoman Empire. Highlights include a series of large blue-and-yellow glazed-brick panels that once lined the processional street and the Ishtar Gate of ancient Babylon.

Tiled Pavilion

Built in 1472 as part of the Topkapı complex, this pavilion was originally used for watching sporting events but now houses the best collection of Seljuk, Anatolian and Ottoman tiles and ceramics in the country.

☑ Top Tips

▶ Unless you have a particular interest in the subject areas, the *Anatolia and Troy Through the Ages* and *Neighbouring Cultures of Anatolia, Cyprus, Syria and Palestine* exhibitions on the upper floors of the Archaeology Museum can easily be given a miss.

▶ If possible, visit the museum and Topkapı Palace on separate days – jamming them into a one-day itinerary may result in museum meltdown.

✗ Take a Break

After spending a few hours admiring the collection here, enjoy panoramic views and a pot of tea at the Set Üstü Çay Bahçesi (p52), a terraced tea garden in nearby Gülhane Park.

To lunch with locals, head to Hocapaşa Sokak (p51) or to the tiny *lokanta* (eatery serving ready-made food) in the courtyard of the historic Caferağa Medresesi (p52).

Saraybumu

Kennedy Cad (Sahil Yolu)

Topkapı Palace

İstanbul Archaeology Museums

Gülhane Park 2 ○

Imperial Gate

Fountain of Sultan ●

Aya ○ 1 İrini

3 ○

Soğukçeşme Sokak

Alemdar Cad

Cafevevy Sk 5

Çıkmazı Soğukçeşme Sk 9

Station İstasyon Arkası Sk

Nöbethane Cad

Taya Hatun Cad

Hüdavendigar Cad

İbn-i Kemal Cad 6

Ebussuud Cad

Gülhane

Hükümet Konağı Sk

Yerebatan Cad 4

Muradiye Cad

Hocapaşa Sk 11

Sirkeci Tram Station

Sirkeci

Ankara Cad

Yalı Köşkü Cad

Hamidiye Cad Sirkeci

EMİNÖNÜ 12 13

Büyük Postane Cad

Aşır Efendi Cad

Köprücü Sk

HOBYAR

Ankara Cad

Cağaloğlu Yokuşu

Cemal Nadir Sk

Hoca Hani Sk

Celal Ferdi Gökçay Sk

Tasvir Sk

CAĞALOĞLU

Prof Kazım İsmail Gürkan Cad

Taşsavak Sk

Alayköşkü Sk

Salkım Söğüt Sk

Ticarethane

ALEMDAR

Şeref Efendi Sk

Cağaloğlu Meydanı

Molla Feneri Sk

Nuruosmaniye Cad

Bab-ı Ali Cad

8

Türbedar Sk

Çatal Çeşme Sk

Sultanahmet

Divan Yolu (Ordu Cad)

200 m
0.1 miles
0
0

For reviews see

◆ Top Sights		p42
○ Sights		p49
⊗ Eating		p51
⊗ Drinking		p52
⊕ Entertainment		p52
⊕ Shopping		p53

Soğukçeşme Sokak

Sights

Aya İrini CHURCH

 Map p48, C4

Commissioned by Justinian around AD 540, this Byzantine church is almost exactly as old as its close neighbour, Aya Sofya. When Mehmet the Conqueror began building Topkapı, the building was within the grounds and was most fortunately retained. Used as an arsenal for centuries, it now functions as an atmospheric concert venue during the İstanbul International Music Festival (http://muzik.iksv.org), held each June. (Hagia Eirene, Church of the Divine Peace; 1st Court, Topkapı Palace; Sultanahmet)

Gülhane Park PARK

2 Map p48, C2

Gülhane Park was once the outer garden of Topkapı Palace, accessed only by the royal court. These days, crowds of locals come here to picnic under the many trees, promenade past the formally planted flower beds and enjoy wonderful views over the Golden Horn and Sea of Marmara from the Set Üstü Çay Bahçesi (p52) in the park's northeastern edge. (Gülhane Parkı; Gülhane)

Soğukçeşme Sokak HISTORIC AREA

3 Map p48, C4

Running between the Topkapı Palace walls and Aya Sofya, this cobbled street is named after the Soğuk Çeşme (Cold

Understand

The Ottoman Empire

Rise of a Dynasty

In the 13th century, a Turkish warlord named Osman (b 1258), known as Gazi (Warrior for the Faith), inherited a small territory from his warlord father. Osman's followers became known as Osmanlıs (Ottomans).

Osman died in 1324. His son Orhan captured Bursa from the Byzantines in 1324, made it his base and declared himself sultan of the Ottoman Empire. Thessaloniki was captured from the Venetians in 1387 and Kosovo from the Serbs in 1389, marking the start of the Ottoman expansion into Europe. Soon, the acquisition of the great city of Constantinople and control of the overland trade routes between Europe and Asia became the dynasty's major objective.

In 1451, 21-year-old Mehmet II became sultan. On 29 May 1453, his army breached Constantinople's massive land walls and took control of the city, bringing the Byzantine Empire to an end. Mehmet was given the title Fatih (Conqueror) and began to rebuild and repopulate the city.

Mehmet died in 1481, but the building boom he kicked off was continued by worthy successors including Sultan Selim I (r 1512–20) and Sultan Süleyman I (r 1520–66), known as 'the Magnificent'.

Decline & Fall

After Süleyman's death, the power of the empire slowly disintegrated. In 1683 the Ottoman army was defeated by the Holy Roman Empire at the Battle of Vienna, marking the end of both its military supremacy and the Ottoman expansion into Europe.

A series of incompetent sultans further weakened the empire. There were some exceptions – Selim III (r 1789–1807), who unsuccessfully attempted to modernise the army, and Mahmut II (r 1808–39), who was finally successful in this aim – but they were few and far between. The 19th-century Tanzimat political reforms ushered in by Mahmut II and continued by Abdülmecid I (r 1839–61) took some strides towards modernity, but were not enough to save the sultanate, which was abolished in 1922. The last of the Osmanlıs to rule as sultan, Mehmet VI (r 1918–22), was expelled from Turkey at this time, and Mustafa Kemal Atatürk became president of the new Turkish Republic.

Fountain) at its southern end. It is home to a row of faux-Ottoman houses functioning as a hotel as well as an undoubtedly authentic restored Byzantine cistern that now operates as the hotel restaurant. (⛴Sultanahmet or Gülhane)

Eating

Cihannüma   TURKISH $$$

4 ✗ Map p48, B4

The view from the top-floor restaurant of this modest hotel is probably the best in the Old City. The Blue Mosque, Aya Sofya, Topkapı Palace, Galata Tower, Dolmabahçe Palace and the Bosphorus Bridge provide a stunning backdrop to a menu showcasing good kebaps (we recommend the *kuzu şiş*), interesting Ottoman-influenced stews and a few vegetarian dishes. (✆212-520 7676; www.cihannumaistanbul.com; And Hotel, Yerebatan Caddesi 18; mezes ₺5-19, mains ₺27-47; ⛴Sultanahmet)

Matbah   OTTOMAN $$$

5 ✗ Map p48, C4

This recent addition to the city's growing number of restaurants specialising in so-called Ottoman Palace Cuisine is well worth a visit. The chef has sourced 375 recipes from the imperial archives and offers an array of dishes, some of which are more successful than others. The surrounds are attractive and there's live Ottoman music on Friday and Saturday nights. (✆212-514 6151; www.matbahrestaurant.com; Ottoman Imperial Hotel,

Caferiye Sokak 6/1; mezes ₺10-22, mains ₺28-48; ⊙lunch & dinner; ⛴Sultanahmet)

Paşazade   TURKISH $$

6 ✗ Map p48, B2

Advertising itself as an *Osmanlı mutfağı* (Ottoman kitchen), Paşazade has long garnered rave reviews from tourists staying in the hotels around Sirkeci. Well-priced dishes are served in the streetside restaurant or on the rooftop terrace (summer only). Portions are large, the food is tasty and service attentive. (✆212-513 3750; www.pasazade.com; İbn-i Kemal Caddesi 5a, Sirkeci; mezes ₺7-18, mains ₺18-28; ⊙lunch & dinner; ⛴Gülhane)

Hafız Mustafa   SWEETS $

7 ✗ Map p48, B2

Making locals happy since 1864, this *şekerlemeleri* (sweets shop) sells delicious *lokum*, baklava, milk puddings,

Local Life
Hocapaşa Sokak

If you're in the Sirkeci neighbourhood at lunchtime, join the locals in this pedestrianised street (Map p48, B2) lined with cheap eateries. *Lokantas* serve *hazır yemek* (ready-made dishes), *köftecis* dish out flavoursome meatballs, *kebapçıs* grill meat to order and the much-loved Hocapaşa *pideci* offers piping-hot pides accompanied by pickles. For more about eating in Sirkeci, visit www.sirkecirestaurants.com.

pastries and *börek* (filled pastries). Put your sweet tooth to good use in the upstairs cafe, or choose a selection of indulgences to take home. (www. hafizmustafa.com; Muradiye Caddesi 51, Sirkeci; börek ₺5, baklava ₺6-7.50, puddings ₺6; ⏰7am-2am; 🚊Sirkeci)

Sefa Restaurant   TURKISH $

8 🍴 Map p48, A4

Locals rate this place near the bazaar highly. It describes its cuisine as Ottoman, but what's really on offer here are *hazır yemek* (ready-made dishes) and kebaps at extremely reasonable prices. You can order from an English menu or choose daily specials from the bain-marie. Try to arrive early-ish for lunch because many of the dishes run out by 1.30pm. No alcohol. (Nuruosmaniye Caddesi 17, Cağaloğlu; portions ₺7-12, kebaps ₺12-18; ⏰7am-5pm; 📶; 🚊Sultanahmet)

Caferağa Medresesi Lokanta & Çay Bahçesi   TURKISH $

9 🍴 Map p48, C4

In this neighbourhood, it's rare to eat in stylish surrounds without being lavishly charged for the privilege. That's why the small *lokanta* in the gorgeous courtyard of this Mimar Sinan–designed *medrese* (Islamic school of higher studies) near Topkapı Palace is such a find. The food's nothing to write home about, but it's fresh and inexpensive. You can enjoy a tea break here, but it's an alcohol-free zone. (Soğukkuyu Çıkmazı 5, off Caferiye Sokak; soup ₺4, portions ₺10; ⏰8.30am-4pm; 🚊Sultanahmet)

Drinking

Set Üstü Çay Bahçesi   TEA GARDEN

10 🚇 Map p48, E1

Come to this terraced tea garden to watch the ferries plying the route from Europe to Asia, while at the same time enjoying an excellent pot of tea accompanied by hot water (such a relief after the usual fiendishly strong Turkish brew). Add a cheap *tost* (toasted sandwich) and you'll be able to make a lunch of it. (Gülhane Park; ⏰9am-10.30pm; 🚊Gülhane)

Entertainment

Hocapaşa Culture Centre   PERFORMING ARTS

11 ⭐ Map p48, B2

Occupying a beautifully converted 550-year-old hamam near Eminönü, this cultural centre stages a one-hour whirling dervish performance for tourists on Friday, Saturday, Sunday, Monday and Wednesday evenings at 7.30pm, and a 1½-hour Turkish dance show on Tuesday and Thursday at 8pm and Saturday and Sunday at 9pm. Note that children under seven are not admitted to the whirling dervish performances. (Hodjapasha Culture Centre; 📞212-511 4626; www. hodjapasha.com; Hocapaşa Hamamı Sokak 3b, Sirkeci; adult/child under 12yr whirling dervish show ₺50/30, Turkish dance show ₺60/40; 🚊Sirkeci)

Gülhane Park (p49)

Shopping

Ali Muhiddin Hacı Bekir
FOOD

12 Map p48, A1

It's obligatory to sample *lokum* while in İstanbul, and one of the best places to do so is at this historic shop, which has been operated by members of the same family for more than 200 years. Buy it *sade* (plain), or made with *cevizli* (walnut), *fıstıklı* (pistachio), *badem* (almond) or *roze* (rose water). There's another store in Beyoğlu. (www.hacibekir.com.tr/eng; Hamidiye Caddesi 83; 8am-8pm Mon-Sat; Eminönü)

Hafız Mustafa
FOOD

13 Map p48, A1

Another excellent place to purchase *lokum*, Hafız Mustafa sells by weight or in prepackaged gift boxes. Best of all, you can taste before buying (within reason, of course). There are other branches in Sirkeci and Sultanahmet. (212-526 5627; Hamidiye Caddesi 84-86; 8am-8pm Mon-Sat, 9am-8pm Sun; Eminönü)

Explore

Grand Bazaar & the Bazaar District

This beguiling neighbourhood, crowned by the historic Grand Bazaar (Kapalı Çarşı), is also home to the smaller but equally historic Spice Bazaar (Mısır Çarşısı), the upmarket shopping street of Nuruosmaniye Caddesi and the frantically busy shopping precinct around Mahmutpaşa Yokuşu. Presiding over the mercantile mayhem is Süleymaniye Mosque, İstanbul's most magnificent Ottoman mosque.

The Sights in a Day

The **Grand Bazaar** (p56) is best visited in the morning, when shopkeepers enjoy gossiping with their neighbours over a glass of tea and are less likely to hassle prospective customers. Wander through this ancient shopping mall for two or three hours, stopping for a coffee or tea at one of its cafes before enjoying lunch at a *lokanta* (eatery serving ready-made food) such as **Bahar Restaurant** (p68) or **Onur Et Lokantası** (p68).

Visit the **Süleymaniye Mosque** (p60), take a break at **Lale Bahçesi** (p69), and then walk down the hill towards the **Spice Bazaar** (p66), popping into the **Rüstem Paşa Mosque** (p63) on the way.

Enjoy a sunset drink on the panoramic terrace of **Zeyrekhane** (p69), followed by a simple dinner at **Fatih Damak Pide** (p67) or **Siirt Fatih Büryan** (p68). For something more sophisticated, take a taxi to **Hamdi Restaurant** (p67), where you can dine on the terrace, and follow up with a drink and nargile (water pipe) at one of the cafes underneath the Galata Bridge.

For a local's day in the Grand Bazaar district, see p62.

👁 Top Sights

Grand Bazaar (p56)

Süleymaniye Mosque (p60)

🔍 Local Life

Between the Bazaars (p62)

💗 Best of İstanbul

Shopping

Abdulla Natural Products (p70)

Derviş (p70)

Ak Gümüş (p72)

Yazmacı Necdet Danış (p72)

Dhoku (p72)

Serhat Geridönmez (p72)

Muhlis Günbattı (p72)

Sevan Bıçakçı (p73)

Getting There

Walk The Grand Bazaar is a short walk from Sultanahmet; the best route is along Yerebatan Caddesi and into pedestrianised Nuruosmaniye Caddesi.

🚋 **Tram** Alight at Beyazıt-Kapalı Çarşı for the Grand Bazaar, Eminönü for the Spice Bazaar, Laleli-Üniversite for the Süleymaniye Mosque and Aksaray for Zeyrek.

🚌 **Bus** Buses 46H or 61B travel between Taksim Sq and Beyazıt Sq, next to the Grand Bazaar.

Top Sights
Grand Bazaar

When Mehmet the Conqueror laid the Kapalı Çarşı's foundation stone in 1455, he gave the imperial imprimatur to a local mercantile tradition that has remained strong ever since. Located in the centre of the Old City, this atmospheric covered market is the heart of İstanbul in much more than a geographic sense – artisans learn their trade here, businessmen negotiate important deals and tourists make a valuable contribution to the local economy (sometimes, it must be said, against their better judgments).

Kapalı Çarşı, Covered Market

👁 Map p64, G4

www.kapalicarsi.org.tr

🕓9am-7pm Mon-Sat

🚋Beyazıt-Kapalı Çarşı

Don't Miss

Nuruosmaniye Mosque & Gate

Built in Ottoman baroque style between 1748 and 1755, this mosque is located on the busy pedestrian route from Cağaloğlu Sq and Nuruosmaniye Caddesi to the bazaar, but is surprisingly peaceful inside. It is located next to one of the major entrances to the Grand Bazaar, the Nuruosmaniye Kapısı (Nuruosmaniye Gate; Gate 1), which is adorned with a golden *tuğra* (crest of the sultan).

Kalpakçılar Caddesi

Shop windows crammed with glittering gold jewellery line both sides of the bazaar's busiest thoroughfare. Originally named after the makers of *kalpakçılars* (fur hats) who had their stores here, it's now full of jewellers who pay up to US$80,000 per year in rent for this high-profile location. In recent years, chain retail stores such as MAC Cosmetics have begun to open outlets along its length, triggering protests by the bazaar's traditional artisans.

Sandal Bedesteni

A majestic space featuring 20 small domes, this 16th-century stone warehouse was built during the reign of Süleyman the Magnificent and has always been used for the storage and sale of fabric. Unfortunately, the current wares don't include the fine *sandal* (fabric woven with silk) that was sold here in the past.

Cevahir (Jewellery) Bedesten

Also known as the Eski (Old) or İç (Inner) Bedesten, this is the oldest part of the bazaar and has always been an area where precious items are stored and sold. These days it's where most of the bazaar's antique stores are located. Also here are top-quality jewellers such as Serhat Geridönmez (p72).

☑ **Top Tips**

▶ Hundreds of traditional artisans work in ateliers in and around the bazaar, but they can be difficult to find and/or visit. If you're keen to do so, consider signing up for a tour of the bazaar conducted by İstanbul Walks (www.istanbulwalks.net); these occur every Saturday.

▶ Bargaining down prices is an accepted practice in traditional carpet, antique and jewellery shops, but the chic homewares shops in the bazaar have fixed prices.

✕ **Take a Break**

Cafes are scattered throughout the bazaar. Our favourites include Şark Kahvesi (p70) and Ethem Tezçakar Kahveci (p70).

For a cheap and tasty lunch, head to Bahar Restaurant (p68), close to the Nuruosmaniye Gate, or Onur Et Lokantası (p68), off nearby Nuruosmaniye Caddesi.

Halıcılar Çarşışı Sokak

The most photogenic street in the bazaar is also the most enticing. Home to designer stores such as Abdulla Natural Products (p70) and Derviş (p70), it also has two of the bazaar's most popular cafes, Ethem Tezçakar Kahveci (p70) and Fes Cafe (p68).

Kuyumcular Caddesi

The name of this street pays tribute to the *kuyumcular* (jewellers) who have always been based here; these days it's the centre of the bazaar's silver merchants. Also here is one of the bazaar's most unusual features, a quaint 19th-century timber structure known as the **Oriental Kiosk**. Once home to the most famous *muhallebici* (milk pudding shop) in the district, it now functions as a jewellery store.

Zincirli Han

Accessed off Kuyumcular Caddesi and named after the *zincirli* (chains) that were once manufactured here, this pretty cobbled caravanserai is now home to one of the bazaar's best-known carpet merchants, Şişko Osman (p72).

Takkeçiler Sokak

This charming street is known for its marble *sebils* (public drinking fountains) and shops selling kilims (pileless woven rugs). These include designer stores such as Dhoku (p72) and EthniCon (p72), which offer kilims featuring modern and avant-garde designs.

Textile Stores

Many of the best textile stores in İstanbul are located on or near the bazaar's major north–south axis – Sipahi Sokak and Yağlıkçılar Caddesi. The crush of shoppers here can occasionally resemble a cavalry charge (in Turkish, *sipahi* means 'cavalry soldier'), but it's worth braving the crowds to visit famous stores such as Yazmacı Necdet Danış (p72), which sells a wonderful array of fabrics.

İç Cebeci Han

This is one of the largest of the bazaar's many caravanserais. In Ottoman times, it would have offered travelling merchants accommodation and a place to do business; these days it's home to artisans' workshops and a popular *kebapçı* called **Kara Mehmet**.

Sahaflar Çarşısı

The 'Secondhand Book Bazaar' has operated as a book and paper market since Byzantine times. At the centre of its shady courtyard is a bust of İbrahim Müteferrika (1674–1745), who printed the first book in Turkey in 1732.

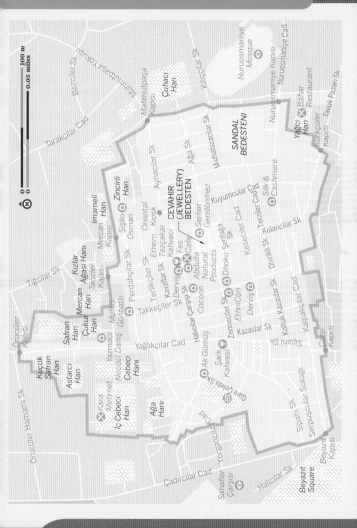

100 m
0.05 miles

Bezciler Sk

Mahmutpaşa Yokuşu

Tarakçılar Cad

Mahmutpaşa Kapısı

Çuhacı Han

Nuruosmaniye Mosque

Kılıçcılar Sk

Nuruosmaniye Kapısı

Nuruosmaniye Cad

Bahar Han Restaurant

Yağcı Han

Kürkçüler Kapısı

Tavuk Pazar Sk

Aynacılar Sk

Ağa Sk

Muhafazacılar Sk

SANDAL BEDESTENI

Zincirli Han

İmameli Han

Mercan Kapısı

Sişko Osman

Oriental Kiosk

Ethem Kahveci

CEVAHIR (JEWELLERY) BEDESTEN

Serhat

Silk & Cashmere

Kuyumcular Cad

Gerdönmez

Tezcakar

Tığcılar Sk

Kızlar Ağası Hanı

Mercan Tacirler Han

Perdahçılar Sk

Terlikçiler Sk

Kavaflar Sk

Fes Cafe

Abdulla Natural Products

Keseciler Cad

Terziler Cad

Divrikli Sk

Kolancılar Sk

Safran Han

Çukur Han

Muhlis Günbattı

Takkeciler Sk

Çarşısı Sk

Dhoku Şerifağa Sk

Cocoon

EthniCon

Derviş

Zennecilet Sk

Kazaslar Sk

Koltuk Kazaslar Sk

Kalpakçılar Cad

Öruculer Kapısı

Küçük Safran Han

Astarcı Han

Yazmacı Necdet Danış Cebeci Han

Yağlıkçılar Cad

Halıcılar Çarşısı Sk

Ak Gümüş

Şark Kahvesi

Gani Çelebi Sk

Kazaslar Sk

Sipahi Sk

Sipahi Sk

Serpuşçular Sk

Kara Mehmet

İç Cebeci Han

Ağa Hanı

Çadırcılar Cad

Yorgancılar Cad

Sahaflar Çarşısı

Halıcılar Sk

Beyazıt Square

Beyazıt Kapısı

Çarşı Kapısı

Öruculer Hamamı Sk

Top Sights
Süleymaniye Mosque

Commissioned by Süleyman I, known as 'The Magnificent', in 1550, the recently restored Süleymaniye was the fourth imperial mosque built in İstanbul and it certainly lives up to its patron's nickname. Crowning one of İstanbul's seven hills, it's the Old City's major landmark and the spiritual hub of the Bazaar District. Though not the largest of the city's Ottoman-era mosques, it is unusual in that many of its original *külliye* (mosque complex) buildings have been retained and sympathetically adapted for re-use.

Map p64, E2

Prof Sıddık Sami Onar Caddesi

Beyazıt-Kapalı Çarşı

Don't Miss

Minarets

The four minarets with their 10 beautiful *şerefes* (balconies) are said to represent the fact that Süleyman was the fourth of the Ottoman sultans to rule the city and the 10th sultan after the establishment of the empire.

Interior

The mosque's architect, Mimar Sinan, incorporated four buttresses into the walls of the building – the result is open, airy and highly reminiscent of Aya Sofya, especially as the dome is nearly as large as the one crowning the great Byzantine basilica. Also notable is the *mihrab* (prayer niche indicating the direction of Mecca), which is decorated with fine İznik tiles.

Tombs

To the right (southeast) of the main entrance is the cemetery, home to the *türbes* (tombs) of Süleyman and his wife Haseki Hürrem Sultan (Roxelana). The tilework in both is superb, as is the stained glass in Roxelana's tomb.

İmaret

The mosque's *imaret* (soup kitchen) is on its northwestern edge. Now occupied by the Dârüzziyafe Restaurant, its tranquil courtyard is a lovely place to enjoy a tea.

Tiryaki Çarşısı

The street facing the mosque's main entrance is now called Prof Sıddık Sami Onar Caddesi, but was formerly known as the Tiryaki Çarşısı (Market of the Addicts) as it was home to tea houses selling opium. These now house popular *fasülye* (bean) restaurants including Kuru Fasülyeci Erzincanlı Ali Baba (p69).

☑ Top Tips

▶ In the garden behind the mosque is a terrace with lovely views of the Golden Horn (Haliç).

▶ The surrounding streets are home to many Ottoman timber houses. To see some, head down Fetva Yokuşu and then veer right into Namahrem Sokak and into Ayrancı Sokak.

▶ Visitors to the mosque must remove their shoes; women should cover their heads with a scarf or shawl.

▶ Avoid visiting at lunchtime on Friday, when weekly sermons and group prayers are held.

✗ Take a Break

For an unusual pick-me-up, head down the streets southwest of the mosque to find Vefa Bozacısı (p70), which has been dispensing *boza*, a drink made with fermented barley, since 1875.

The courtyard of Lale Bahçesi (p69) is a relaxing spot to enjoy a tea and nargile.

Local Life
Between the Bazaars

Locals outnumber tourists by a generous margin in the crowded and cacophanous streets surrounding the Grand and Spice Bazaars. Here, housewives source bargains, street vendors hawk fresh fruit and pastries, and the atmosphere crackles with good-humoured energy.

....

1 Mahmutpaşa Kapısı

Exit the Grand Bazaar by this gate (Gate 18) and you'll find yourself on the busy thoroughfare of Mahmutpaşa Yokuşu, which runs down to the Spice Bazaar and is home to shops selling everything from wedding dresses to woollen socks, coffee cups to circumcision outfits

2 Delicious Döner Kebaps

Ask any shopkeeper in the Grand Bazaar about who makes the best döner kebap in the immediate area,

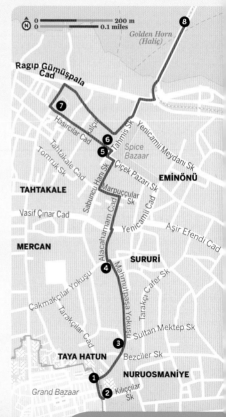

and they are likely to give the same answer: 'Şahin Usta, of course!' Grab one to go from **Dönerci Şahin Usta** (Kılıççılar Sokak 7, Nuruosmaniye; döner kebap ₺10; ⊙10am-3pm Mon-Sat; ⛟Çemberlitaş).

❸ Mahmutpaşa Hamamı

One of the oldest Ottoman hamams in the city (it dates from 1476), this building was converted into a down-market shopping centre a decade or so ago. Its domed ceiling, stained-glass windows and marble floor offer a glimpse of its former glory.

❹ Islamic Chic

In Bebek and Beyoğlu the fashion might be for tight jeans, revealing jackets and chunky jewellery, but here in the Old City there's little make-up and even less flesh on show. Wildly popular **Armine** (www.armine.com; Mahmutpaşa Yokuşu 181, Eminönü; ⊙10am-6pm Mon-Sat; ⛟Eminönü) is where Zara style meets the headscarf.

❺ Turkish Coffee to Take Home

Tahmis Sokak on the western edge of the Spice Bazaar hosts a jumble of stalls selling slabs of pungent farmhouse cheese, tubs of olives and mounds of *biber salçası* (hot pepper paste). Also here is the flagship store of Turkey's most famous coffee purveyor, **Kurukahveci Mehmet Efendi** (www.mehmetefendi.com/eng; cnr Tahmis Sokak & Hasırcılar Caddesi, Eminönü; ⊙9am-6pm Mon-Sat; ⛟Eminönü).

❻ Hasırcılar Caddesi

The shops lining this narrow street running parallel to the Golden Horn sell everything from teapots to toothbrushes. Stock up on provisions or grab a snack at **Namlı** (www.namlipastirma.com.tr; Hasırcılar Caddesi 14-16, Eminönü; ⊙6.30am-7pm Mon-Sat; 🍴; ⛟Eminönü), a deli known for its huge selection of *pastırma* (spiced, air-dried beef), speciality cheeses and ready-made mezes.

❼ Rüstem Paşa Mosque

This diminutive mosque is a gem. Dating from 1560, it was designed by Mimar Sinan for Rüstem Paşa, son-in-law and grand vizier of Süleyman the Magnificent. A showpiece of the best Ottoman architecture and tilework, it's accessed via stairs off Hasırcılar Caddesi or off a side street to the right (north). Avoid visiting during prayer times, when local shopkeepers worship here.

❽ Galata Bridge

This İstanbul icon carries a constant flow of locals crossing between Beyoğlu and Eminönü, hopeful anglers trailing their lines into the waters below, and a changing procession of street vendors hawking everything from fresh-baked *simits* (sesame-encrusted bread rings) to Rolex rip-offs. Consider enjoying a beer and nargile while watching the ferries ply the surrounding waters.

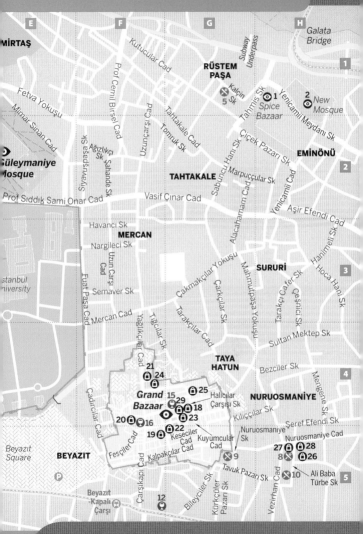

E

MİRTAŞ

Fetva Yokuşu

Mimar Sinan Cad

Süleymaniye
Mosque

Prof Sıddık Sami Onar Cad

İstanbul
University

Beyazıt
Square

BEYAZIT

F

Kutucular Cad

Prof Cemil Birsel Cad

Ağızlıkçı Sk

Sıyavuşpaşa Sk

Şahande Sk

Uzunçarşı Cad

Tahtakale Cad

Tomruk Sk

TAHTAKALE

Vasif Çınar Cad

Havancı Sk

MERCAN

Nargileci Sk

Uzun Çarşı Cad

Semaver Sk

Mercan Cad

Fuat Paşa Cad

Yağlıkçılar Cad

Tığcılar Sk

Tarakçılar Cad

Çadırcılar Cad

21
24

Grand
Bazaar

15
29

20
16

19
22

Keseciler
Cad

Feşçiler Cad

Kalpakçılar Cad

Çarşıkapı Cad

Bileyiciler Sk

Beyazıt
-Kapalı
Çarşı

12

G

Subway
Underpass

RÜSTEM
PAŞA

Kalçın
Sk 5

1
Spice
Bazaar

Çiçek Pazarı Sk

Sabuncu Hanı Cad

Marpuççular Sk

Alacahamam Cad

Çakmakçılar Yokuşu

Çarkçılar Sk

Mahmutpaşa Yokuşu

TAYA
HATUN

25
Halıcılar
Çarşısı Sk

18
23

Kuyumcular
Cad

9

Tavuk Pazarı Sk

Kürkçüler
Pazarı Sk

H

Galata
Bridge

Tahmis Sk

Yenicamii Meydanı Sk

2
New
Mosque

EMİNÖNÜ

Yenicamii Cad

Aşir Efendi Cad

Hanımeli Sk

Hoca Hanı Sk

SURURİ

Tarakçı Cafer Sk

Çeşnici Sk

Sultan Mektep Sk

Bezciler Sk

NURUOSMANİYE

Kılıçılar Sk

Nuruosmaniye
Sk

Nuruosmaniye Cad

Mengene
Sk

Seref Efendi Sk

27
8

28
26

Vezirhan Cad

10
Ali Baba
Türbe Sk

Sights

Spice Bazaar
MARKET

1 ⊙ Map p64, H1

Vividly coloured pyramids of spices, ornate displays of jewel-like *lokum* (Turkish delight) and trays of artfully arranged dried fruit provide eye candy for the thousands of tourists and locals who visit the Ottoman-era Spice Bazaar everyday. Also known as the Mısır Çarşısı (Egyptian Market), it's perennially crowded, always noisy, and an essential stop on every itinerary. At the time of research, the bazaar was opening on Sundays in the high season but shopkeepers were uncertain if this would continue. (Mısır Çarşısı, Egyptian Market; ⊙8am-6pm Mon-Sat, 9am-6pm Sun; 🚋Eminönü)

New Mosque
MOSQUE

2 ⊙ Map p64, H1

Only in İstanbul would a 400-year-old mosque be called 'New'. Dating from 1597, its design references both the Blue Mosque and the Süleymaniye Mosque, with a large forecourt and a square sanctuary surmounted by a series of semidomes crowned by a grand dome. The interior is richly decorated with gold leaf, coloured İznik tiles and carved marble. (Yeni Camii; Yenicamii Meydanı Sokak, Eminönü; 🚋Eminönü)

Monastery of Christ Pantokrator
MONASTERY

3 ⊙ Map p64, B1

This Byzantine monastery originally comprised two churches, a library, a cistern, a hospital and a chapel, but only one church and a cistern remain (currently being restored). The church became a mosque after the Conquest. It is the second-largest surviving Byzantine religious structure in the city after Aya Sofya. (Zeyrek Camii; İbadethane Sokak, Zeyrek; 🚋Aksaray)

Understand
Ottoman Hans

Built by rich merchants, *hans* (caravanserais) enabled caravans to unload and trade their spices, furs, silks and slaves right in the thick of the bazaar action. Typically two- to three-storey arcaded buildings set around a court-yard where animals could be housed, they differed from Persian-style caravanserais in that they were used as storage and trading spaces as well as for short-term accommodation. Although *hans* are found all over Turkey, the concentration in İstanbul is unrivalled, a testament to the city's importance as a trading-route hub. Sadly, most are in a dilapidated state today.

Spice Bazaar

Eating

Fatih Damak Pide PIDE $

 Map p64, A2

It's worth making the trek to this *pideci* overlooking the İtfaiye Yanı Parkı Karşısı (Fire Station Park) near the Aqueduct of Valens, a 4th-century limestone aqueduct that's one of the city's most distinctive landmarks. Fatih Damak's reputation for making the best Karadeniz (Black Sea)–style pide on the Historic Peninsula is well deserved, and the free pots of tea served with meals are a nice touch. Great pide, great staff, great choice! (Büyük Karaman Caddesi 48, Zeyrek; pide ₺8-12; ⏰11am-11pm; 🚊Aksaray)

Hamdi Restaurant KEBAPS $$

5 🍴 Map p64, G1

Hamdi Arpacı's empire dates to the 1960s, when he established a street stand near the Spice Bazaar selling tasty kebaps made according to recipes from his hometown Urfa, in Turkey's southeast. Over the years his kebaps became so popular with locals that he acquired this nearby building, which has phenomenal views from its top-floor terrace. Booking is advisable. (☏212-528 8011; www.hamdirestorant.com.tr; Kalçın Sokak 17, Eminönü; mezes ₺7-15, kebaps ₺20-28, dessert ₺7-15; 🚊Eminönü)

Siirt Fatih Büryan
TURKISH $

6   Map p64, A1

Those who enjoy investigating regional cuisines should head to this eatery in the Kadın Pazarı (Women's Market) near the Aqueduct of Valens. It specialises in two dishes that are a speciality of the southeastern city of Siirt: *büryan* (lamb slow-cooked in a pit) and *perde pilavi* (chicken and rice cooked in pastry). Both are totally delicious. No alcohol. (İtfaiye Caddesi 20a, Zeyrek; büryan ₺11, perde pilavi ₺10; Aksaray)

Sur Ocakbaşı
KEBAP $$

7   Map p64, A1

Indulge in some peerless people-watching while enjoying the grilled

meats at this popular place in the Kadın Pazarı. The square is always full of locals shopping or enjoying a gossip, and tourists were a rare sight before Anthony Bourdain filmed a segment of *No Reservations* here and blew Sur's cover. (212-533 8088; www.surocakbasi.com; İtfaiye Caddesi 27, Zeyrek; kebaps ₺11-20; Aksaray)

Fes Cafe
CAFE $$

8   Map p64, H5

After a morning spent trading repartee with the touts in the Grand Bazaar, you'll be in need of a respite. Fortunately, this stylish cafe just outside the Nuruosmaniye Gate is an excellent place to relax over lunch or a coffee. Popular choices include Turkish coffee (served with a piece of *lokum*), homemade lemonade and generously proportioned bowls of pasta. There's also a branch inside the bazaar, set in a rough-stone den on Halıcılar Çarşışı Sokak. (www.fescafe.com; Ali Baba Türbe Sokak 25, Nuruosmaniye; sandwiches ₺12-19, salads ₺16-18, pasta ₺17-19; closed Sun; Çemberlitaş)

Bahar Restaurant
TURKISH $

9   Map p64, G5

Our favourite eatery in the Grand Bazaar precinct, tiny Bahar ('Spring') is popular with local shopkeepers and is always full, so arrive early to score a table. Dishes change daily and with the season – try the delicious lentil soup, tasty *hünkar beğendi* (lamb stew served on a bed of roasted

---

Local Life
Fish Sandwiches

The city's favourite fast-food treat is undoubtedly the *balık ekmek* (fish sandwich), and the most atmospheric place to try one is at the Eminönü end of the Galata Bridge. Here, in front of fishing boats tied to the quay, are a number of stands where mackerel fillets are grilled, crammed into fresh bread and served with salad; a generous squeeze of bottled lemon is optional but recommended. A sandwich will set you back a mere ₺5 or so, and is delicious accompanied by a glass of the *şalgam* (sour turnip juice) sold by nearby pickle vendors.

and puréed aubergine) or creamy macaroni. No alcohol. (Yağcı Han 13, off Nuruosmaniye Sokak, Nuruosmaniye; soup ₺4, dishes ₺9-15; ⏰11am-4pm Mon-Sat; 🍴; 🚇Çemberlitaş)

Onur Et Lokantası TURKISH, KEBAP $

10 🍴 Map p64, H5

An excellent neighbourhood eatery, this place close to the Grand Bazaar grills succulent kebaps to order and displays an array of daily dishes in its bain-marie. Of these, the aubergine dishes are particularly tasty. No alcohol. (Shop 7, Ali Baba Türbe Sokak 21, Nuruosmaniye; dishes ₺9-16; ⏰8am-4pm Mon-Sat; 🚇Çemberlitaş)

Kuru Fasülyeci
Erzincanlı Ali Baba TURKISH $

11 🍴 Map p64, D2

Join the crowds of hungry locals at this long-time institution opposite the Süleymaniye Mosque. It's been dishing up its signature *kuru fasulye* (Anatolian-style white beans cooked in a spicy tomato sauce) since 1924 and they're delicious when accompanied by pilaf (rice) and *turşu* (pickles). Next door, Kanaat Fasülyeci is nearly as old and serves up more of the same. No alcohol. (www.kurufasulyeci.com; Prof Sıddık Sami Onar Caddesi 11, Süleymaniye; beans with pilaf & pickles ₺10; ⏰7am-7pm; 🍴; 🚇Laleli-Üniversite)

Drinking

Erenler Çay Bahçesi TEA GARDEN

12 🍷 Map p64, F5

Set in the vine-covered courtyard of the Çorlulu Ali Paşa Medrese, this nargile cafe near the Grand Bazaar is a favourite with students from nearby İstanbul University. (Yeniçeriler Caddesi 35, Beyazıt; ⏰7am-midnight; 🚇Beyazıt-Kapalı Çarşı)

Lale Bahçesi TEA GARDEN

13 🍷 Map p64, D2

In a sunken courtyard that was once part of the Süleymaniye *külliye,* this charming outdoor tea house is always full of students from the nearby theological college and İstanbul University, who come here to sit on cushioned seats under trees and relax while watching the pretty fountain play. It's one of the cheapest places in the area to enjoy a tea and nargile. (Şifahane Caddesi, Süleymaniye; ⏰9am-11pm; 🚇Laleli-Üniversite)

Zeyrekhane CAFE

14 🍷 Map p64, B1

This lovely cafe opposite the Byzantine Monastery of Christ Pantokrator has a dining space filled with antique handicrafts as well as a garden terrace offering magnificent views of the Golden Horn and Süleymaniye Mosque. Though the menu includes choices such as sandwiches and *köfte* (meatballs), we recommend coming here to enjoy the view over a coffee or sunset aperitif. (www.zeyrekhane.com; İbadethane Arkası Sokak 10, Zeyrek; ⊙9.30am-10pm Tue-Sun; 🚇Aksaray)

Ethem Tezçakar Kahveci   CAFE

15 🚇 Map p64, G4

Bekir Tezçakar's family has been at the helm of this tiny coffee shop for four generations. Smack bang in the middle of the bazaar's most glamorous retail strip, its traditional brass-tray tables and wooden stools stand in stark contrast to the Western-style Fes Cafe, opposite. (Halıcılar Çarşışı Sokak, Grand Bazaar; ⊙8.30am-7pm Mon-Sat; 🚇Beyazıt-Kapalı Çarşı)

Şark Kahvesi   CAFE

16 🚇 Map p64, F4

The Şark's arched ceiling betrays its former existence as part of a bazaar street; years ago some enterprising *kahveci* (coffee maker) walled up several sides and turned it into a cafe. Located on one of the bazaar's major thoroughfares, it's popular with both stallholders and tourists. (Oriental Coffeeshop; Yağlıkçılar Caddesi 134, Grand Bazaar; ⊙8.30am-7pm Mon-Sat; 🚇Beyazıt-Kapalı Çarşı)

Vefa Bozacısı   BOZA BAR

17 🚇 Map p64, B2

This famous *boza* bar was established in 1875 and locals still flock here to drink the viscous tonic, which is made from water, sugar and fermented barley. The mucous-coloured beverage has a reputation for building up strength and virility – it won't be to everyone's taste, but the bar's pretty interior is worth a visit in its own right. (www.vefa.com.tr; cnr Vefa & Katip Çelebi Caddesis, Molla Hüsrev; boza ₺2.50; ⊙8am-midnight; 🚇Laleli-Üniversite)

Shopping

Abdulla Natural Products   TEXTILES, BATHWARE

18 🔒 Map p64, G4

The first of the Western-style designer stores to appear in this ancient marketplace, Abdulla sells top-quality cotton bed linen and towels, handspun woollen throws from Eastern Turkey, cotton *peştemals* (bath wraps) and pure olive-oil soap. There's another store in the Fes Cafe in Nuruosmaniye. (Halıcılar Çarşışı Sokak 62, Grand Bazaar; ⊙9am-7pm Mon-Sat; 🚇Beyazıt-Kapalı Çarşı)

Derviş   TEXTILES, BATHWARE

19 🔒 Map p64, F5

Gorgeous raw cotton and silk *peştemals* share shelf space with traditional Turkish dowry vests and engagement dresses. If these don't take your fancy, the pure olive-oil soaps and old hamam bowls are sure to step into the breach. There's another store in the bazaar at Halıcılar Çarşışı Caddesi 51. (www.dervis.com; Keseciler Caddesi 33-35, Grand Bazaar; ⊙9am-7pm Mon-Sat; 🚇Beyazıt-Kapalı Çarşı)

Understand

İstanbul in Print

This colourful and complex city has inspired writers throughout history, and continues to do so today. Local luminaries including Orhan Pamuk and Elif Şafak set most of their novels here, and many foreign writers have used the city as a literary setting.

Local Writers

İrfan Orga's 1950 masterpiece *Portrait of a Turkish Family* is among the best writing about the city ever published, as is *A Mind at Peace* (1949) by Ahmet Hamdi Tanipar. Elif Şafak's *The Flea Palace* (2002) and *The Bastard of Istanbul* (2006) are both acclaimed novels set in İstanbul.

Nobel laureate Orhan Pamuk has set most of his novels here, including *Cevdet Bey & His Sons* (1982), *The White Castle* (1985), *The Black Book* (1990), *The New Life* (1995), *My Name is Red* (1998) and *The Museum of Innocence* (2009). In 2005 he published a memoir, *Istanbul: Memories of a City*.

Literary Visitors

Foreign novelists and travel writers have long tried to capture the magic and mystery of İstanbul in their work. One of the earliest to do so was French novelist Pierre Loti, whose novel *Aziyadé* (1879) introduced Europe to Loti's almond-eyed Turkish lover and to the mysterious and all-pervasive attractions of the city itself. Another notable work from this period is *Constantinople* (1878) by Italian writer Edmondo De Amicis.

Historical novels set here include *The Rage of the Vulture* (Barry Unsworth; 1982), *The Stone Woman* (Tariq Ali; 2001), *The Calligrapher's Night* (Yasmine Ghata; 2006) and *The Dark Angel* (Mika Waltari; 1952).

Set in the modern era, Alan Drew's 2008 novel *Gardens of Water* is about two families in the aftermath of the devastating earthquake that struck western Turkey (including İstanbul's outskirts) in 1999.

The city also features as the setting for some great crime novels, including Barbara Nadel's Inspector İkmen novels (the first of which is *Belshazzar's Daughter*, 1999); Jason Goodwin's Yashim the Ottoman Investigator novels (*The Janissary Tree*, 2006); Jenny White's Kamil Paşa novels (*The Sultan's Seal*, 2006); and Mehmet Murat Somer's Hop-Çıkı-Yaya series of gay crime novels (*The Prophet Murders*, 2008).

Ak Gümüş HANDICRAFTS

20 🔒 Map p64, F4

Specialising in Central Asian tribal arts, this delightful store stocks an array of felt toys and hats, as well as jewellery and other objects made using coins and beads. (Gani Çelebi Sokak 8, Grand Bazaar; ⏰9am-7pm Mon-Sat; 🚇Beyazıt-Kapalı Çarşı)

Yazmacı Necdet Danış TEXTILES

21 🔒 Map p64, F4

Fashion designers and buyers from every corner of the globe know that when in İstanbul, this is where to come to source top-quality textiles. It's crammed with bolts of fabric of every description – shiny, simple, sheer and sophisticated – as well as *peştemals,* scarves and clothes. Next-door Murat Danış is part of the same operation. (Yağlıkçılar Caddesi 57, Grand Bazaar; ⏰9am-7pm Mon-Sat; 🚇Beyazıt-Kapalı Çarşı)

Dhoku CARPETS

22 🔒 Map p64, G5

One of the new generation of rug stores opening in the bazaar, Dhoku (meaning 'texture') sells artfully designed wool kilims in resolutely modernist designs. Its sister store, **EthniCon**, opposite this store, sells similarly stylish rugs in vivid colours and can be said to have started the current craze in contemporary kilims. (www.dhoku.com; Takkeçiler Sokak 58-60, Grand Bazaar; ⏰9am-7pm Mon-Sat; 🚇Beyazıt-Kapalı Çarşı)

Serhat Geridönmez JEWELLERY

23 🔒 Map p64, G4

There are plenty of jewellers in the Grand Bazaar, but few sell objects as gorgeous as the expertly crafted copies of Hellenistic, Roman and Byzantine pieces on offer at this tiny store. (Şerifağa Sokak 69, Old Bazaar, Grand Bazaar; ⏰9am-7pm Mon-Sat; 🚇Beyazıt-Kapalı Çarşı)

Muhlis Günbattı TEXTILES

24 🔒 Map p64, F4

One of the most famous stores in the bazaar, Muhlis Günbattı specialises in *suzani* fabrics from Uzbekistan. These beautiful bedspreads, tablecloths and wall hangings are made from fine cotton embroidered with silk. As well as the textiles, Muhlis Günbattı stocks top-quality carpets, brightly coloured kilims and a small range of antique Ottoman fabrics richly embroidered with gold. (www.muhlisgunbatti.net; Perdahçılar Sokak 48, Grand Bazaar; ⏰9am-7pm Mon-Sat; 🚇Beyazıt-Kapalı Çarşı)

Şişko Osman CARPETS

25 🔒 Map p64, G4

The Osmans have been in the rug business for four generations and are rated by many as the best dealers in the bazaar. Certainly, their stock is a cut above many of their competitors. Most of the rugs on sale are dowry pieces and all have been hand woven and coloured with vegetable dyes. (Fatty Osman; www.siskoosman.com.tr; Zincirli Han 15, Grand Bazaar; ⏰9am-7pm Mon-Sat; 🚇Beyazıt-Kapalı Çarşı)

Sevan Bıçakçı
JEWELLERY

26 Map p64, H5

Inspired by the monuments and history of his much-loved İstanbul, flamboyant jeweller Sevan Bıçakçı creates wearable art that aims to impress. His flagship store is in the Kutlu Han near the Grand Bazaar's Nuruosmaniye Gate. (www.sevanbicakci.com; Gazi Sinan Paşa Sokak 16, Nuruosmaniye; ⊙10am-6pm Mon-Sat; 🚊Çemberlitaş)

Sofa
ART, JEWELLERY

27 Map p64, H5

Investigation of Sofa's artfully arranged clutter reveals an eclectic array of pricey jewellery, prints, textiles, calligraphy, Ottoman miniatures and contemporary Turkish art. (www.kashifsofa.com; Nuruosmaniye Caddesi 53, Nuruosmaniye; ⊙9.30am-7pm Mon-Sat; 🚊Çemberlitaş)

Silk & Cashmere
CLOTHING

28 Map p64, H5

The Nuruosmaniye branch of this popular chain sells cashmere and silk-cashmere-blend cardigans, jumpers, tops and shawls. All are remarkably well priced considering their quality. There's another, smaller, store on Kalpakçılar Caddesi inside the Grand Bazaar. (www.silkcashmere.com; Nuruosmaniye Caddesi 69, Nuruosmaniye; ⊙9.30am-7pm Mon-Sat; 🚊Çemberlitaş)

Cocoon
RUGS, TEXTILES

29 Map p64, G4

This small branch of the very stylish Sultanahmet-based textile and rug business specialises in jewellery and items made from felt. (www.cocoontr.com; Halıcılar Çarşışı Sokak 38, Grand Bazaar; ⊙9am-7pm Mon-Sat; 🚊Beyazıt-Kapalı Çarşı)

Top Sights
Kariye Museum (Chora Church)

Getting There

Kariye Museum is 5km west of Sultanahmet.

🚌 **Bus** 31E, 32, 36K & 38E from Eminönü, 87 from Taksim, Edirnekapı stop.

⛴ **Ferry** Golden Horn (Haliç) from Eminönü

İstanbul has more than its fair share of Byzantine monuments, but few are as drop-dead gorgeous as this mosaic-laden church. Nestled in the shadow of Theodosius II's monumental land walls and now a museum overseen by the Aya Sofya curators, it receives a fraction of the visitor numbers that its big sister attracts but offers an equally fascinating insight into Byzantine art. Virtually all of the interior decoration – the famous mosaics and the less renowned but equally striking frescoes – dates from 1312.

Don't Miss

Inner Narthex

Highlights in the second of the inner corridors include the *Khalke Jesus*, which shows Christ and Mary with two donors. The southern dome features a stunning depiction of Jesus and his ancestors (the *Genealogy of Christ*) and the northern dome features a serenely beautiful mosaic of Mary and the Baby Jesus surrounded by her ancestors.

Nave

In the nave are mosaics of Christ; of Mary and the Baby Jesus; and of the *Assumption of the Blessed Virgin* – turn around to see this, as it's over the main door you just entered. The 'infant' being held by Jesus is actually Mary's soul.

Parecclesion

This side chapel was built to hold the tombs of the church's founder and relatives. It's decorated with frescoes depicting scenes taken from the Old Testament; most deal with the themes of death and resurrection. The striking painting in the apse shows a powerful Christ raising Adam and Eve out of their sarcophagi, with saints and kings in attendance.

The Chora's Patron

Most of the interior decoration was funded by Theodore Metochites, a poet and man of letters who was auditor of the treasury under Emperor Andronikos II (r 1282–1328). One of the museum's most wonderful mosaics, found above the door to the nave in the inner narthex, depicts Theodore offering the church to Christ.

---

kariye.muze.gov.tr

Kariye Camii Sokak, Edirnekapı

admission ₺15

⊘9am-7pm Thu-Tue Apr-Oct, to 4.30pm Nov-Mar

☑ Top Tips

▶ The best way to visit Edirnekapı is to take the Golden Horn (Haliç) ferry, alight at Ayvansaray and walk up the hill alongside the historic city walls. To return to Sultanahmet, consider walking down Fevzi Paşa Caddesi through the fascinating suburb of Fatih.

✗ Take a Break

Dishes devised for the palace kitchens at Topkapı, Edirne and Dolmabahçe are on offer at **Asitane** (☏212-635 7997; www.asitanerestaurant.com; starters ₺12-18, mains ₺26-42; ⊘11am-midnight; ☏) in the next-door Kariye Hotel.

Enjoy a glass of tea on the terrace of the Kariye Pembe Köşk in the plaza overlooking the museum.

Explore

İstiklal Caddesi & Beyoğlu

This is the city's high-octane hub of eating, drinking and entertainment, full of crowded restaurants, glamorous rooftop bars and live-music venues. Built around the pedestrianised boulevard of İstiklal Caddesi, it incorporates bohemian residential districts such as Çukurcuma and Cihangir, bustling entertainment enclaves such as Asmalımescit, and historically rich pockets such as Galata and Karaköy.

The Sights in a Day

☀ Begin your day at **Taksim Sq** (p79), the symbolic heart of both Beyoğlu and the modern city. From here, wander down **İstiklal Caddesi** (p78), being sure to visit the **Balık Pazarı** (p79), **SALT Beyoğlu** (p79) and **ARTER** (p79). Stop for coffee at **Manda Batmaz** (p92), then visit Orhan Pamuk's **Museum of Innocence** (p88) and the surrounding district of Çukurcuma, home to many of the city's antique shops.

☀ Dedicate your afternoon to art. Begin at the **İstanbul Modern** (p80), enjoying lunch and a Bosphorus view at the **İstanbul Modern Cafe/Restaurant** (p90) before checking out the collection of Turkish and international art. Afterwards, sample the baklava at **Karaköy Güllüoğlu** (p88) before taking a taxi to the **Pera Museum** (p87) to admire its Orientalist art.

☾ Beyoğlu is known for its rooftop bars, so kick off your evening at **Mikla** (p92), **360** (p93) or **Leb-i Derya Richmond** (p93). Then move on to a traditional eatery to eat, drink and make merry *à la Turka* – **Asmalı Cavit** (p88), **Sofyalı 9** (p90) and **Zübeyir Ocakbaşı** (p89) are all great options. Kick on to a club, or wind down at the **Tophane Nargile Cafes** (p93).

For a local's day in Galata, see p82.

◉ Top Sights

◯ Local Life

♥ Best of İstanbul

Eating

Drinking & Nightlife

Getting There

🚋 **Tram** The tram from Sultanahmet stops at Eminönü, crosses the Galata Bridge and then stops at Karaköy, Tophane, Fındıklı and Kabataş.

Funicular It's a steep uphill walk from all tram stops to İstiklal, so most commuters use the funiculars that link Karaköy with Tünel Sq and Kabataş with Taksim Sq.

Top Sights
İstiklal Caddesi

Once called the Grand Rue de Pera but renamed İstiklal (Independence) in the early years of the Republic, Beyoğlu's premier boulevard is a perfect metaphor for 21st-century Turkey. A long pedestrianised strip full of shops, cafes, cinemas and cultural centres, it showcases İstanbul's Janus-like personality, embracing modernity one minute and happily bowing to tradition the next. Come here to experience the city as the locals do, promenading the street's length and taking advantage of its excellent eating, drinking and shopping opportunities.

Independence Ave

◉ Map p84, C2

Don't Miss

Taksim Square
Named after the 18th-century stone *taksim* (water storage unit) on its western side, this busy square is home to a chaotic bus terminus, an architecturally significant cultural centre and an often-overlooked monument to the founding of the Republic.

Çiçek Pasajı
Built in 1876 and decorated in Second Empire style, the Cité de Pera building once housed a shopping arcade and apartments. The arcade is now known as the Çiçek Pasajı (Flower Passage) and is full of boisterous *meyhanes* (taverns).

Balık Pazarı
Next to the Çiçek Pasajı, Galatasaray's fish market is full of small stands selling *midye tava* (skewered mussels fried in hot oil), *kokoreç* (skewered lamb or mutton intestines seasoned and grilled over charcoal) and fresh produce.

SALT Beyoğlu
Occupying a former apartment building dating from the 1850s, this three-level **cultural centre** (www.saltonline.org/en; İstiklal Caddesi 136; ⏲noon-8pm Tue-Sat, 10.30am-6pm Sun; 🚋Karaköy, then funicular to Tünel) offers exhibition spaces, a walk-in cinema and a bookshop.

ARTER
This four-floor **contemporary arts space** (www.arter.org.tr; İstiklal Caddesi 211; ⏲11am-7pm Tue-Thu, noon-8pm Fri-Sun; 🚋Karaköy, then funicular to Tünel) has been neck-and-neck with the Garanti Bank's SALT venues in the race for the accolade of most exciting new arts venue in the city. In our view, the result is tied.

☑ **Top Tips**

▶ Start at Taksim Sq and walk down İstiklal, ending your exploration in historic Galata, where you can sample some of the local lifestyle (p82).

▶ The neighbourhoods within Beyoğlu all have distinct and fascinating characters. Be sure to veer off İstiklal during your perambulation to explore districts such as Cihangir, Çukurcuma, Asmalımescit and Galata.

✗ **Take a Break**

For one of the best Turkish coffees in the city, head to tiny Manda Batmaz (p92), where the *kahveci* (coffee maker) has been perfecting his art for two decades.

Hazzo Pulo Çay Bahçesi (p93) is a popular tea house hidden in a cobbled courtyard near Galatasaray Sq.

Top Sights
İstanbul Modern

In recent years İstanbul's contemporary art scene has boomed. Facilitated by the active cultural philanthropy of the country's industrial dynasties – many of which have built extraordinary arts collections – museum buildings are opening nearly as often as art exhibitions. İstanbul Modern Sanat Müzesi, funded by the Eczıbaşı family, is the big daddy of them all. Opened with great fanfare in 2005, this huge converted shipping terminal has a stunning location right on the shores of the Bosphorus at Tophane and is easily accessed by tram from Sultanahmet.

 Map p84, D6

www.istanbulmodern.org

Meclis-i Mebusan Caddesi, Tophane

adult/student/under 12yr ₺15/8/free

⊙10am-6pm Tue, Wed & Fri-Sun, to 8pm Thu

🚋Tophane

Don't Miss

Downstairs Galleries
The permanent exhibition upstairs is interesting, but the real drawcards at this gallery are the temporary exhibitions on the ground floor. Check out what is showing in the main temporary gallery (it's always good), the photography gallery and the pop-up exhibition spaces.

False Ceiling
A visually arresting work by Richard Wentworth, this installation of Turkish and Western books floating overhead plays with ideas of cultural closeness and difference. Created between 1995 and 2005, it dominates the central space downstairs.

Permanent Collection
The Eczcıbaşı family's collection of works by prominent 20th-century Turkish artists is showcased on the entrance floor, offering an insight into the country's modern art from its beginnings to the present day. Also on this floor is a small space with pieces by high-profile Turkish and international contemporary artists working in the mediums of painting, sculpture and video.

The Road to Tate Modern
Erkan Özgen and Şener Özmen's 2003 video is an ironic reworking of Cervantes' *Don Quixote*. You'll find it in the upstairs projection room.

Gift Shop
The museum's gift shop stocks a tempting array of jewellery, homewares and stationery made by local artisans, as well as a range of art books, magazines and CDs.

☑ Top Tips

▶ If your visit coincides with the staging of the İstanbul Biennial (www.iksv.org), check the website for special events and launches.

▶ Book a table in advance if you plan to have lunch in the restaurant, and specify that you would like a table with a view.

▶ If you're visiting with a child, ask about the dedicated kids audio guide, which can be hired for ₺4.

✗ Take a Break

The İstanbul Modern Cafe/Restaurant (p90) is one of the best lunch spots in the city. Its view of the Bosphorus and over to the Historic Peninsula is wonderful, and its menu of Italian and Turkish dishes will please most palates. There's also good espresso coffee and a decent list of wines by the glass.

Local Life
An Afternoon in Galata

This ancient and highly atmospheric neighbourhood has a very different feel to the rest of the city, perhaps due to its history as a sequestered settlement built and heavily fortified by Genoese traders in the 14th century. Its bohemian credentials are similarly unique, with galleries, bars and edgy boutiques scattered among the handsome apartment buildings that line its narrow cobbled streets.

....

1 People-Watching on Galata Square

The square surrounding the Galata Tower is a popular local gathering place. Enjoy a tea with the locals at **Cafe Gündoğdu** while watching young people from across the city congregate on the pavement and outdoor benches surrounding the landmark tower.

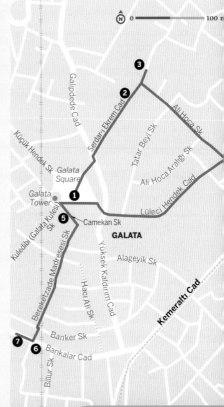

❷ Shopping in Serdar-ı Ekrem Caddesi

One of the city's most interesting and attractive enclaves, this narrow cobbled street is home to avant-garde boutiques showcasing creations by the best of the city's young designers. Be sure to visit **Bahar Korçan** (www.baharkorcan.org; Serdar-ı Ekrem Sokak 9, Galata; ⊗closed Sunday; 🚋Karaköy) and **Arzu Kaprol** (www.arzukaprol.net; Serdar-ı Ekrem Sokak 22, Galata; 🚋Karaköy).

❸ Boho Central

Members of the local art and fashion communities are regulars at **Mavra** (Serdar-ı Ekrem Caddesi 31a, Galata; ⊗8am-midnight; 🚋Karaköy, then funicular to Tünel), a laid-back cafe with a thrift-shop chic decor; it serves good, cheap home-style cooking. At the end of the day, locals wind down at the *très* glamorous **Le Fumoir** (www.georges.com; Georges Hotel, Serdar-ı Ekrem Caddesi 24, Galata; ⊗8am-1am; 🚋Karaköy) bar in the Georges Hotel.

❹ Designer Wares

Interior designer Emel Güntaş is one of İstanbul's style icons, and her recently opened shops **Dear East** (www.deareast.com; Lüleci Hendek Sokak 35, Tophane; ⊗10.30am-7pm Mon-Sat; 🚋Tophane) and **Hiç** (www.hiccrafts.com; Lüleci Hendek Sokak 35, Tophane; ⊗10.30am-7pm Mon-Sat; 🚋Tophane) on the border of Galata and Tophane are favourite destinations for the city's design mavens. The artisan-made stock includes furniture, cushions, carpets, kilims (pileless woven rugs), silk scarves, woollen shawls, porcelain, felt crafts, paintings and photographs.

❺ Turkish Style

Head back to Galata Square and wander down Camekan Sokak, a winding street of boutiques selling Anatolian-influenced designer handicrafts. Don't miss the jewellery and T-shirts at **Lâl** (www.lalistanbul.com; Camekan Sokak 4c, Galata; ⊗10.30am-8pm; 🚋Karaköy) and the silver-plated homewares at **İroni** (www.ironi.com.tr; Camekan Sokak 4e, Galata; ⊗10.30am-8pm; 🚋Karaköy).

❻ Camondo Stairs

This sculptural set of stairs is one of Galata's most famous landmarks. Commissioned and paid for by the famous banking family of the same name, it leads down to Bankalar Caddesi, centre of the city's prosperous banking industry in the 19th century and now a busy commercial precinct.

❼ A Cultural Interlude

Housed in a magnificent 1892 bank building designed by Alexandre Vallaury and cleverly adapted by local architectural firm Mimarlar Tasarım, the cutting-edge **SALT Galata** (www.saltonline.org/en; Bankalar Caddesi 11, Karaköy; ⊗noon-8pm Tue-Sat, 10.30am-6pm Sun; 🚋Karaköy) houses a busy exhibition space, auditorium and arts research library. The glamorous rooftop bar-restaurant is a perfect spot to finish your afternoon's exploration.

Meclis-i Mebusan

TOPHANE
○24
✕15
◉ İstanbul Modern

Başhorus Şivral Boğazici (Bosphorus)

For reviews see
◆ Top Sights p78
⊙ Sights p86
✕ Eating p88
⊙ Drinking p92
⊙ Entertainment p95
⊙ Shopping p96

200 m
0.1 miles

Tophane İskele Cad
Ali Paşa Medresesi Sk
Denizciler
Murabe Sk
Kemankeş Cad
◉46 Necatibey Cad
Ali Paşa Değirmeni Sk
Muntahane Cad
✕12
✕9
ℹ

1. Set Sk
Karabaş Cad
Karabaş Deresi Sk
Cami Sk
Tophane ⊞
Fevzi Sk
Kumbaracı Yokuşu
Hacı Mimi Külhanı Sk
⊞49
Kemeralti Cad

Golden Horn (Haliç)

Arapoğlan Sk
Jewish Museum ⊙8 of Turkey ✕11
KARAKÖY
Gümrük Sk
Karaköy

Şah Kulu
Bostan Sk
⊞47 ◉3 Galata Sk
Mevlevi Museum
Seydan-i Ekrem Cad
Ali Hoca Sk
Tatar Bey Sk
Lüleci Hendek Cad
Galata Galipdede Cad
⊞27

TÜNEL
Ⓜ ⊞44
Şişhane ⊞
Tünel Square
Şişhane
⊙33 41

Galata Tower
Küçük Hendek Sk
◉2
⊞45
Büyük Hendek Cad
Kulediba (Galata Kulesi) Sk
Laleli Çeşme Sk
Okçu Musa Cad

GALATA
Perçemli Sk
✕1 of Turkey
Bilitur Sk

Banker Sk
Bankalar Cad
✕13

Karaköy Rıhtım Cad
Karaköy Square
Karaköy
Galata Bridge
Karaköy Fish Market
Tersane Cad
Kürekçiler Cad

Sights

Jewish Museum of Turkey
MUSEUM

1 Map p84, B7

Housed in the ornate 19th-century Zulffaris synagogue near the Galata Bridge, this museum was established in 2001 to commemorate the 500th anniversary of the arrival of the Sephardic Jews in the Ottoman Empire. Its modest but extremely well-intentioned collection comprises photographs, papers and objects that document the mostly harmonious coexistence between Jews and the Muslim majority in this country. (500

Yil Vakfi Türk Musevileri, The Quincentennial Foundation Museum of Turkish Jews; www.muze500.com; Perçemli Sokak, Karaköy; admission ₺10; 10am-4pm Mon-Thu, to 2pm Fri & Sun; Karaköy)

Galata Tower
LANDMARK

2 Map p84, A6

The cylindrical Galata Tower stands sentry over the approach to 'new' İstanbul. Constructed in 1348, it was the tallest structure in the city for centuries, and it still dominates the skyline north of the Golden Horn (Haliç). Its vertiginous upper balcony offers 360-degree views of the city, but we're not convinced that the view (though spectacular) justifies the steep admis-

Understand
Jewish İstanbul

The history of the Jews in Turkey is as long as it is fascinating. In the late 15th century, Isaac Sarfati, Chief Rabbi of Edirne, wrote the following to brethren in Germany: 'Brothers and teachers, friends and acquaintances! I, Isaac Sarfati, proclaim to you that Turkey is a land wherein nothing is lacking, and where, if you will, all shall yet be well with you… Here, every man may dwell at peace under his own vine and fig tree.' At around the same time, Sultan Beyazıt II proclaimed '…the Jews of Spain should not be refused, but rather be welcomed with warm feelings.' Alas, this enlightened state didn't last through the centuries, and Jewish Turks were made to feel considerably less welcome when racially motivated 'wealth taxes' were introduced in 1942 and violence against Jews and other minorities was unleashed in 1955, prompting many families to flee the country. More recently, Islamist terrorists have bombed synagogues on a number of occasions.

Approximately 23,000 Jews currently live in Turkey, with most residing in İstanbul. Sephardic Jews make up approximately 96% of this number, while the rest are primarily Ashkenazic. Today there are a total of 16 synagogues in İstanbul, all of which are Sephardic except for one. For a list of these, see www.jewish-europe.net/turkey/en/synagogue.

Pera Palace Hotel (p88)

sion cost. (Galata Kulesi; www.galatatower.net; Galata Meydanı, Galata; admission ₺12; ⊙9am-8pm; 🚋Karaköy)

Galata Mevlevi Museum MUSEUM

3 🎯 Map p84, B5

The *semahane* (whirling-dervish hall) at the centre of this *tekke* (dervish lodge) was erected in 1491 and renovated in 1608 and 2009. It is part of a complex including a *meydan-ı şerif* (courtyard), *çeşme* (drinking fountain), *türbesi* (tomb) and *hamuşan* (cemetery). The oldest of six historic Mevlevihaneleri (Mevlevi *tekkes*) remaining in İstanbul, the complex was converted into a museum in 1946. (Galata Mevlevihanesi Müzesi; www.mekder.org; Galipdede Caddesi 15, Tünel; admission ₺5; ⊙9am-4.30pm Tue-Sun; 🚋Karaköy, then funicular to Tünel)

Pera Museum MUSEUM

4 🎯 Map p84, B3

Head to this classy museum to admire works from Suna and İnan Kıraç's splendid collection of paintings featuring Turkish Orientalist themes. A changing program of thematic exhibitions provides fascinating glimpses into the Ottoman world from the 17th to the early 20th century. (Pera Müzesi; www.peramuzesi.org.tr; Meşrutiyet Caddesi 65, Tepebaşı; adult/student/child under 12yr ₺10/7/free; ⊙10am-7pm Tue-Sat, noon-6pm Sun; 🚋Karaköy, then funicular to Tünel)

Museum of Innocence   MUSEUM

5 ⊙ | Map p84, C4

His status as a Nobel laureate deserves respect, but we feel obliged to say that Orhan Pamuk is a bit cheeky to charge visitors to this long-anticipated museum/piece of conceptual art the same entrance fee that is charged at Aya Sofya and Topkapı Palace, especially as the exhibits here will only resonate with visitors who have read and enjoyed the eponymously titled novel that it celebrates. (www.masumiyetmuzesi.org; Dalgıç Çıkmazı 2, off Çukurcuma Caddesi, Çukurcuma; admission ₺25; ⊙10am-6pm Tue-Sun, till 9pm Fri; 🚋Tophane)

Pera Palace Hotel   HISTORIC BUILDING

6 ⊙ | Map p84, A4

The Pera Palas was a project of Georges Nagelmackers, the Belgian entrepreneur who linked Paris and Constantinople with his famous Orient Express train service. The 1892 building has undergone a €23 million restoration in recent years and claims to have regained its position as İstanbul's most glamorous hotel. Its bar, patisserie, tea lounge and restaurant are open to the public. (Pera Palas Otell; www.perapalace.com; Meşrutiyet Caddesi 52, Tepebaşı; 🚋Karaköy, then funicular to Tünel)

Eating

Asmalı Cavit   MEYHANE $$

7 🍴 | Map p84, B4

Cavit Saatcı's place is quite possibly the best *meyhane* in the city. The old-fashioned interior gives no clue as to the excellence of the food on offer. Standout dishes include *yaprak ciğer* (liver fried with onions), *patlıcan salatası* (eggplant salad), *muska böreği* (filo pastry stuffed with beef and onion) and *kalamar tava* (fried calamari). Bookings essential. (Asmalı Meyhane; 📞212-292 4950; Asmalımescit Sokak 16, Asmalımescit; mezes ₺6-20, mains ₺18-24; 🚋Karaköy, then funicular to Tünel)

Karaköy Güllüoğlu   SWEETS, BÖREK $

8 🍴 | Map p84, C7

This Karaköy institution has been making customers deliriously happy since 1947. Head to the register and order a *porsiyon* (portion) of whatever baklava takes your fancy (*fıstıklı* is pistachio, *cevizli* walnut and *sade* plain), preferably with a glass of tea. Then hand your ticket over to the servers. The *börek* (filled pastry) here is good, too. (www.karakoygulluoglu.com; Kemankeş Caddesi, Karaköy; baklava ₺4-7, börek ₺6; ⊙8am-11pm; 🚋Karaköy)

Lokanta Maya   MODERN TURKISH $$$

9 🍴 | Map p84, C7

Critics and chowhounds alike are raving about the Aegean-accented dishes created by chef Didem Şenol at her stylish restaurant near the Karaköy docks. You'll need to book for dinner; lunch is cheaper and more casual. (☏212-252 6884; www.lokantamaya.com; Kemankeş Caddesi 35a, Karaköy; mezes ₺11-28, mains ₺26-35; ⏱lunch Mon-Sat, dinner Tue-Sat, brunch Sun; ✔; ☲Karaköy)

Zübeyir Ocakbaşı
KEBAPS **$$**

10 ✖ Map p84, D1

Every morning, the chefs at this popular *ocakbaşı* (fireside kebap restaurant) prepare the fresh, top-quality meats to be grilled over their handsome copper-hooded barbecues that night. Their offerings are famous throughout the city, so booking a table is essential. (☏212-293 3951; www.zubeyir ocakbasi.com; Bekar Sokak 28; mezes ₺4-6, kebaps ₺10-20; ⏱noon-1am; ☲Kabataş, then funicular to Taksim)

Meze by Lemon Tree
MODERN TURKISH **$$$**

11 ✖ Map p84, A4

Chef Gençay Üçok creates some of the most interesting – and delicious – modern Turkish food found in the city. Come to his small restaurant opposite the Pera Palace Hotel to sample triumphs such as monkfish casserole or grilled lamb sirloin with baked potatoes and red beets; both are sure to be holiday highlights. Bookings are essential. (☏212-252 8302; www.mezze. com.tr; Meşrutiyet Caddesi 83b, Tepebaşı; mezes ₺8-25, mains ₺26-36; ☲Karaköy, then funicular to Tünel)

Karaköy Lokantası
MEYHANE, LOKANTA **$$**

12 ✖ Map p84, C7

Known for its gorgeous tiled interior, genial owner and bustling vibe, Karaköy Lokantası serves tasty, well-priced food to its loyal local clientele. It functions as a *lokanta* (eatery serving ready-made food) during the day, but at night it morphs into a *meyhane*, with slightly higher prices. Bookings are essential for dinner. (☏212-292 4455; Kemankeş Caddesi 37a, Karaköy; mezes ₺6-10, portions ₺7-12, grills ₺11-16; ⏱dinner daily, lunch Mon-Sat; ✔; ☲Karaköy)

Ca' d'Oro
ITALIAN **$$**

13 ✖ Map p84, A7

The glamorous rooftop restaurant at the SALT Galata cultural centre serves *molto buono* Italian staples such as pasta, pizza and risotto, but is most memorable for its extraordinary view over the Golden Horn to the Historic

---

☑ Top Tip

Culinary Backstreets

Culinary Backstreets (www. culinarybackstreets.com) is an excellent blog investigating the traditional food culture of the city and a great resource for those interested in seeking out local eateries and food districts. The team that puts it together also conducts excellent foodie tours – check the website for details.

Peninsula. Vegetarians will appreciate the generous array of suitable options on the menu. (☎212-243 8292; www.istanbuldoors.com; Bankalar Caddesi 11, Galata; starters ₺10-29, pizzas ₺15-21, mains ₺18-55; ☺lunch & dinner Tue-Sun; ☑; ☒Karaköy)

Antiochia
ANATOLIAN $$

14 ☒ Map p84, A4

Dishes from the southeastern city of Antakya (Hatay) are the speciality at this tiny (read cramped) restaurant. Mezes are dominated by wild thyme, pomegranate syrup, olives, walnuts and tangy homemade yoghurt, and the kebaps are equally flavoursome. There's a 20% discount at lunch. (☎212-292 1100; www.antiochiaconcept.com; Minare Sokak 21a, Asmalımescit; mezes ₺8-10, mains ₺13-27; ☺lunch Mon-Fri, dinner Mon-Sat; ☒Karaköy, then funicular to Tünel)

İstanbul Modern Cafe/Restaurant
INTERNATIONAL $$$

15 ☒ Map p84, D6

The cafe-restaurant at İstanbul's pre-eminent contemporary art museum offers an 'industrial arty' vibe and great views over the Bosphorus when there are no cruise ships moored in front. The pasta is homemade, pizzas are Italian-style and service is slick – all of which makes for a happy dining experience. You'll need to book ahead to score a table on the terrace. (☎212-292 2612; Meclis-i Mebusan Caddesi, Tophane; pizzas ₺19-28, pasta ₺19-33, mains ₺28-55; ☺10am-midnight; ☑; ☒Tophane)

Changa
MODERN INTERNATIONAL $$$

16 ☒ Map p84, E2

A number of eateries in İstanbul attempt fusion cuisine, but few do it well; this sophisticated restaurant is one that does. Most diners opt for the 10-course tasting menu (₺135 per person, minimum 2 people), but you can also order à la carte. In summer, the action moves to the glamorous **MüzedeChanga** (p109) on the Bosphorus. (☎212-249 1348; www.changa-istanbul.com; Sıraselviler Caddesi 47, Taksim; starters ₺25-30, mains ₺35-55; ☺6pm-1am Mon-Sat Nov-Jun; ☒Kabataş, then funicular to Taksim)

Sofyalı 9
MEYHANE $$

17 ☒ Map p84, A5

Tables at this *meyhane* are hot property on a Friday or Saturday night, and no wonder. The food is fresh and tasty, and the atmosphere is convivial. Stick to mezes rather than ordering mains – choose cold dishes from the waiter's tray and order hot ones from the menu. (☎212-245 0362; Sofyalı Sokak 9, Asmalımescit; mezes ₺2.50-10, mains ₺13-25; ☺closed Sun; ☒Karaköy, then funicular to Tünel)

Kafe Ara
CAFE $$

18 ☒ Map p84, B3

This casual cafe is named after its owner, legendary local photographer Ara Güler. It occupies a converted garage with tables and chairs spilling out into a wide laneway opposite the

A Beyoğlu *meyhane* (tavern)

Galatasaray Lycée and serves an array of well-priced salads, sandwiches and Turkish staples such as *sigara böreği* (deep-fried cigar-shaped pastries filled with cheese and potato). No alcohol. (Tosbağ Sokak 8a, Galatasaray; sandwiches ₺15-20, salads ₺15-23, grills ₺19-24; ☺7.30am-midnight Mon-Thu, to 1am Fri & Sat, to 10pm Sun; ◫Kabataş, then funicular to Taksim)

Asmalı Canım Ciğerim ANATOLIAN $

19 ✖️ Map p84, A4

The name means 'my soul, my liver', and this small place behind the Ali Hoca Türbesi specialises in grilled liver served with herbs, *ezme* (spicy tomato sauce) and grilled vegetables. No alcohol, but *ayran* (a salty yoghurt drink) is the perfect accompaniment. (Minare Sokak 1, Asmalımescit; 5 skewers ₺12; ◫Karaköy, then funicular to Tünel)

Mikla MODERN TURKISH $$$

20 ✖️ Map p84, A4

Local celebrity chef Mehmet Gürs is a master of Mod Med, and the Turkish accents on the menu here makes his food memorable. Extraordinary views, luxe surrounds and professional service complete the experience. Be sure to have a drink on the rooftop bar before your meal. (☎212-293 5656; www.miklarestaurant.com; Marmara Pera Hotel, Meşrutiyet Caddesi 15, Tepebaşı; appetisers ₺25-38, mains ₺51-79; ☺dinner; ◫Karaköy, then funicular to Tünel)

○ Local Life
Manda Batmaz

İstanbullus love to sip Cemil Pilik's viscous yet smooth Turkish coffee, and flock to this tiny **coffee house** (Map p84, B3; Olivia Geçidi 1a, off İstiklal Caddesi; ⏱9.30am-midnight; 🚇Karaköy, then funicular to Tünel) behind the Barcelona Cafe & Patisserie on İstiklal Caddesi.

Journey
INTERNATIONAL, CAFE $$

21 🍴 Map p84, D4

This bohemian lounge-cafe in the expat enclave of Cihangir serves a great range of Mediterranean comfort foods including sandwiches, soups, pizzas and pastas. (www.journeycihangir.com; Akarsu Yokuşu 21a, Cihangir; soups ₺7-9, sandwiches ₺14-19, mains ₺15-39; ⏱9am-2am; ✒; 🚇Kabataş, then funicular to Taksim)

Jash
ANATOLIAN $$

22 🍴 Map p84, E4

Armenian specialities such as *topik* (a cold meze made with chickpeas, pistachios, onion, flour, currants, cumin and salt) make an appearance on the menu of this bijou *meyhane* in trendy Cihangir. Come on the weekend, when an accordian player entertains diners. (☎212-244 3042; www.jashistanbul.com; Cihangir Caddesi 9, Cihangir; mezes ₺8-20, mains ₺20-42; ⏱lunch & dinner; 🚇Kabataş, then funicular to Taksim)

Demeti
MEYHANE $$

23 🍴 Map p84, E4

This modern *meyhane* has a friendly feel and simple but stylish decor. Reservations are a must if you want one of four tables on the terrace, which have an unimpeded Bosphorus view. There's occasional live music. (☎212-244 0628; www.demeti.com.tr; Şimşirci Sokak 6, Cihangir; mezes ₺5-20, mains ₺16-25; ⏱4pm-2am Mon-Sat; 🚇Kabataş, then funicular to Taksim)

Drinking

Mikla
BAR

It's worth overlooking the occasional uppity service at this stylish rooftop bar (see 20 🍴 Map p84, A4) to enjoy what could well be the best view in İstanbul. (www.miklarestaurant.com; Marmara Pera Hotel, Meşrutiyet Caddesi 15, Tepebaşı; ⏱from 6pm Mon-Sat summer only; 🚇Karaköy, then funicular to Tünel)

Tophane Nargile Cafes
NARGILE CAFE

24 🍷 Map p84, D6

This atmospheric row of nargile cafes behind the Nusretiye Mosque is always packed with locals enjoying tea, nargile and snacks. Follow your nose to find it – the smell of apple tobacco is incredibly enticing. (off Necatibey Caddesi, Tophane; ⏱24hr; 🚇Tophane)

MiniMüzikHol

CLUB, LIVE MUSIC

25 Map p84, D3

The mothership for inner-city hipsters, MMH is a small, slightly grungy venue near Taksim that hosts live sets by local and international musicians midweek and the best dance party in town on weekends. (MMH; www. minimuzikhol.com; Soğancı Sokak 7, Cihangir; ⏱Wed-Sat 10pm-late; 🚊Kabataş, then funicular to Taksim)

360

BAR

26 Map p84, B3

İstanbul's most famous bar, and deservedly so. If you can score one of the bar stools on the terrace you'll be happy indeed – the view is truly extraordinary. It morphs into a club after midnight on Friday and Saturday, when a cover charge of around ₺40 applies. (www.360istanbul.com; 8th fl, İstiklal Caddesi 163; ⏱noon-2am Mon-Thu & Sun, 3pm-4am Fri & Sat; 🚊Karaköy, then funicular to Tünel)

Leb-i Derya

BAR

27 Map p84, B5

On the top floor of a dishevelled building off İstiklal, Leb-i Derya has wonderful views across to the Old City and down the Bosphorus, meaning that seats on the small outdoor terrace or at the bar are highly prized. (www.lebiderya.com; 6th fl, Kumbaracı Yokuşu 57, Galata; ⏱4pm-2am Mon-Thu, to 3am Fri, 10am-3am Sat, to 2am Sun; 🚊Karaköy, then funicular to Tünel)

Münferit

BAR

28 Map p84, C4

When this book went to print, this up-market bar-restaurant designed by the Autoban Design Partnership was the most glamorous destination in town. The bar serves expertly made cocktails and good wine by the glass. (Yeni Çarşı Caddesi 19, Galatasaray; 🚊Kabataş, then funicular to Taksim)

Leb-i Derya Richmond

BAR, RESTAURANT

29 Map p84, B4

This sleek younger sister of perennial favourite Leb-i Derya attracts an older, more cashed-up crowd. Its decor and views are hard to beat. (📞212-243 4375; www.lebiderya.com; 6th fl, Richmond Hotel, İstiklal Caddesi 445; ⏱11am-2am Mon-Thu, to 3am Fri & Sat, to 2am Sun; 🚊Karaköy, then funicular to Tünel)

Local Life
Hazzo Pulo Çay Bahçesi

There aren't as many traditional tea houses in Beyoğlu as there are on the Historic Peninsula, so this ramshackle **çay bahçesi** (Map p84, B3; Tarihi Hazzo Pulo Pasaji, off İstiklal Caddesi; ⏱9am-midnight; 🚊Karaköy, then funicular to Tünel) in a picturesque cobbled courtyard off İstiklal Caddesi is a local favourite. Order from the waiter and then pay at the small cafe near the narrow arcade entrance.

Baylo
BAR, RESTAURANT

30 🚇 Map p84, A4

The much-anticipated reopening of the Pera Palace Hotel in the lower section of Asmalımescit has been accompanied by a boom in glamorous bistro-bars in its immediate vicinity. Of these, Baylo is undoubtedly the best. (www.baylo.com.tr; Meşrutiyet Caddesi 107a, Tepebaşı; ⊘6.30pm-1am Mon-Thu, to 2.30am Fri & Sat; 🚋Karaköy, then funicular to Tünel)

Kiki
CLUB, CAFE

31 🚇 Map p84, D3

Cool cafe by day and hip bar-club by night, Kiki has a loyal clientele who enjoy its pizzas, burgers, drinks and music (DJs and live sets). Regulars head to the rear courtyard. (www.kiki.com.tr; Sıraselviler Caddesi 42 , Cihangir; ⊘closed Sun; 🚋Kabataş, then funicular to Taksim)

Club 17
GAY

32 🚇 Map p84, D1

Rent boys outnumber regulars at this narrow bar. At closing time, the crowd spills out into the street to make final hook-up attempts possible. It's quiet during the week but jam-packed late on Friday and Saturday. (Zambak Sokak 17; ⊘11pm-5am; 🚋Kabataş, then funicular to Taksim)

X Bar
BAR

33 🚇 Map p84, A5

High culture meets serious glamour at this bar on the top floor of the İstanbul Foundation for Culture and Arts (İKSV) building. Come for a sunset aperitif or two – the Golden Horn view is simply extraordinary. (www.xrestaurantbar.com; 7th fl, Sadı Konuralp Caddesi 5, Şişhane; ⊘9am-midnight Sun-Wed, to 4am Thu-Sat)

Bigudi Cafe
GAY

34 🚇 Map p84, D1

The first lesbian-exclusive venue in Turkey, Bigudi is frequented by lipstick lesbians on Saturday nights, when it is resolutely off-limits to non-females. Fridays are open to gay men and the transgendered. To find it, look for the Altin Plak cafe on the ground floor. (www.bigudiproject.net; terrace fl, Mis Sokak 5; ⊘11pm-4am Fri & Sat; 🚋Kabataş, then funicular to Taksim)

NuTeras
BAR, RESTAURANT

35 🚇 Map p84, B3

This bar-restaurant attracts a fashionable crowd to the rooftop terrace of the NuPera Building. Its expansive Golden Horn view is spectacular and the after-dinner club scene is trés chic. (www.nupera.com.tr/nuteras; 6th fl, NuPera Building, Meşrutiyet Caddesi 67, Tepebaşı; ⊘noon-1am Mon-Thu, noon-4am Fri & Sat summer only; 🚋Karaköy, then funicular to Tünel)

Dogzstar
CLUB

36 🚇 Map p84, C3

It's a three-storey affair, but the compact size (300 persons max) makes for an acoustic powerhouse. The crowd comprises budding fans or hard-core followers of featured up-and-coming bands or DJs. The owners give the collected (modest) cover charges to performers and also charge reasonable drink prices. Bravo! There's a terrace where clubbers cool off in summer. (www.dogzstar.com; Kartal Sokak 3, Galatasaray; ☉closed Sun; 🚋Kabataş, then funicular to Taksim)

Tek Yön
GAY

37 🚇 Map p84, E2

This sleek club features the city's largest gay dance floor as well as a garden popular with smokers and cruisers. The core clientele is hirsute and fashion-challenged. Cuddly bears abound. (1st fl, Siraselviler Caddesi 63, Taksim; ☉10pm-4am; 🚋Kabataş, then funicular to Taksim)

Entertainment

Galata Mevlevi Museum
WHIRLING-DERVISH PERFORMANCE

38 ⭐ Map p84, B5

The 15th-century *semahane* at this *tekke* is the venue for a *sema* (ceremony) held most Sundays during the year. Tickets are only available on the day of the performance and often sell out – your best bet is to purchase tickets well ahead of the performance (the ticket office opens at 9am). (Galata Mevlevihanesi Müzesi; Galipdede Caddesi 15, Tünel; admission ₺40; ☉performances 4pm Sun; 🚋Karaköy, then funicular to Tünel)

Whirling-dervish performance

Babylon
LIVE MUSIC, CLUB

39 ⭐ Map p84, A4

İstanbul's pre-eminent live-music venue offers an eclectic program featuring big-name international music acts, particularly during the festival season. Most of the action occurs in the concert hall, but there's also a lounge with DJ. (www.babylon. com.tr; Şehbender Sokak 3, Asmalımescit; ☉9.30pm-2am Tue-Thu, 10pm-3am Fri & Sat, club closed summer; 🚋Karaköy, then funicular to Tünel)

Local Life
Türkü Evleri

Hasnun Galip Sokak in Galatasaray is home to a number of *Türkü evleri*, Kurdish-owned bars where musicians perform live, emotion-charged *halk meziği* (folk music) in front of groups of locals who sing along with gusto. Venues such as **Munzur Cafe & Bar** (Map p84, D2; www.munzurcafe bar.com; Hasnun Galip Sokak, Galatasaray; ⏰1pm-4am Tue-Sun, music from 9pm; 🚇Kabataş, then funicular to Taksim) and **Toprak** (Map p84, D2; 📞212-293 4037; www.toprakturkubar.tr.gg/ana-sayfa.htm; Hasnun Galip Sokak, Galatasaray; ⏰4pm-4am, show from 10pm) are particularly busy on Friday and Saturday nights.

Nardis Jazz Club JAZZ

40 ⭐ Map p84, A6

Named after a Miles Davis track, this intimate venue near the Galata Tower is run by jazz guitarist Önder Focan and his wife Zuhal. Performers include gifted amateurs, local jazz luminaries and visiting international artists. It's small, so you'll need to book if you want a decent table. (📞212-244 6327; www.nardisjazz.com; Kuledibi Sokak 14, Galata; ⏰9.30pm-12.30am Mon-Thu, 9.30pm-1.30am Fri & Sat, closed August; 🚇Karaköy)

Salon LIVE MUSIC

41 ⭐ Map p84, A5

This intimate performance space in the İstanbul Foundation for Culture & Arts (İKSV) building hosts live

contemporary music (mainly jazz), lectures and theatrical performances; check the website for program and booking details. Before or after the show, be sure to have a drink at X Bar (p94), in the same building. (📞212-334 0700; www.saloniksv.com; İstanbul Foundation for Culture & Arts, Nejat Eczacıbaşı Building, Sadi Konuralp Caddesi 5, Şişhane; 🚇Karaköy, then funicular to Tünel)

Shopping

A La Turca CARPETS, ANTIQUES

42 🔒 Map p84, D3

Antique Anatolian kilims and textiles are stacked alongside top-drawer Ottoman antiques in this fabulous shop in Çukurcuma. This is the best area in the city to browse for antiques and curios, and A La Turca is probably the most interesting of all its retail outlets. Ring the doorbell to gain entrance. (www.alaturcahouse.com; Faikpaşa Sokak 4, Çukurcuma; ⏰10.30am-7.30pm Mon-Sat; 🚇Kabataş, then funicular to Taksim)

Beyoğlu Olgunlaşma Enstitüsü HANDICRAFTS

43 🔒 Map p84, D2

This is the ground-floor retail outlet/gallery of the Beyoğlu Olgunlaşma Enstitüsü, a textile school where students in their final year of secondary school learn crafts such as felting, embroidery, knitting and lacemaking. It sells well-priced examples of their work, giving them a taste of its commercial possibilities. (www.beyogluolgunlasma.k12.tr; İstiklal Caddesi 28; ⊙9am-5pm Mon-Fri; 🚋Kabataş, then funicular to Taksim)

Artrium
ART, JEWELLERY

44 🔒 Map p84, A5

Crammed with antique ceramics, calligraphy, maps, prints and jewellery, this Aladdin's cave of a shop is most notable for the exquisite miniatures by Iranian artist Haydar Hatemi. (www.artrium.com.tr; Tünel Geçidi 7, Tünel; ⊙closed Sun; 🚋Karaköy, then funicular to Tünel)

Hammam
BATHWARE

45 🔒 Map p84, A6

The wonderful smell of naturally scented soap greets shoppers as they enter this small shop hidden in a street in the shadow of the Galata Tower. The traditional laurel- and olive-oil soaps on offer are very well priced, as are the attractive cotton and silk *peştemals* (bath wraps) and bathrobes. (www.hammam.com.tr; Kule Çıkmazı, Galata; ⊙11am-8pm; 🚋Karaköy)

Selda Okutan
JEWELLERY

46 🔒 Map p84, C6

Selda Okutan's sculptural pieces featuring tiny naked figures have the local fashion industry all aflutter. Come to her design studio in Tophane to see what the fuss is about. (www.

seldaokutan.com; Ali Paşa Değirmeni Sokak 10a, Tophane; ⊙closed Sun; 🚋Tophane)

Lale Plak
MUSIC

47 🔒 Map p84, B5

This small shop is crammed with CDs including a fine selection of Turkish classical, jazz and folk music. It's a popular hang-out for local musicians. (Galipdede Caddesi 1, Tünel; ⊙9.30am-7.30pm Mon-Sat, 10.30am-7pm Sun; 🚋Karaköy, then funicular to Tünel)

Leyla Eski Eşya Pazarlama
CLOTHING

48 🔒 Map p84, D3

If you love old clothes, you'll adore this boutique. Filled to the brim with piles of vintage embroidery and outfits, it's a rummager's delight. It stocks everything from 1950s taffeta party frocks to silk-embroidery cushion covers that would've been at home in the Dolmabahçe Palace linen cupboard. (Altıpatlar Sokak 6, Çukurcuma; ⊙11am-5.30pm; 🚋Kabataş, then funicular to Taksim)

SIR
CERAMICS

49 🔒 Map p84, B5

Ceramics produced in İstanbul can be pricey, but the attractive hand-painted plates, platters, bowls and tiles sold at this small atelier are exceptions to the rule. (www.sircini.com; Serdar-i Ekrem Sokak 66, Galata; ⊙closed Sun; 🚋Karaköy, then funicular to Tünel)

Explore

Dolmabahçe Palace & Ortaköy

The stretch of Bosphorus shore between Beşiktaş and Ortaköy is home to the splendid Ottoman-era buildings of Dolmabahçe, Yıldız and Çırağan. North of this picturesque palace precinct is the famous 'Golden Mile', a string of upmarket nightclubs running between the waterside suburbs of Ortaköy and Kuruçeşme, once humble fishing villages and now prime pockets of real estate.

The Sights in a Day

☀ Beat the queues by arriving at **Dolmabahçe Palace** (p100) as soon as it opens. After taking at least one of the guided tours, enjoy a tea at the waterside *çay bahçesi* (tea garden) and then catch a bus or taxi to Ortaköy for lunch at the **House Cafe** (p103) or **Zuma** (p106).

☀ Those who haven't yet reached Ottoman overload should head to **Yıldız Park** (p105) to visit the chalet built by order of Sultan Abdül Hamit II. Others can take a **Bosphorus Tour** (p103) to Anadolu Hisarı and back, or enjoy a drink or two on the glamorous pool terrace at the **Çırağan Palace Kempinski Hotel** (p107).

☾ Sample some of the local seafood at **Sıdıka** (p106) before making your way to one of the clubs along the Golden Mile. If you're appropriately dressed and don't mind sending a hefty tip the doorman's way, you'll soon be partying with the glitterati against the illuminated backdrop of the monumental Bosphorus Bridge.

For a local's day in Ortaköy, see p102.

👁 Top Sights
Dolmabahçe Palace (p100)

🔍 Local Life
Weekend Wander in Ortaköy (p102)

💜 Best of İstanbul

Architecture
Dolmabahçe Palace (p100)

Çırağan Palace (p105)

Eating
Sıdıka (p105)

Nightlife
Reina (p106)

Sortie (p106)

Shopping
Lokum (p107)

Haremlique (p107)

Getting There

🚌 **Bus** Lines 22, 22RE and 25E travel from Kabataş along Çırağan, Muallim Naci and Kuruçeşme Caddesis and on to the Bosphorus suburbs. Lines 40, 40T or 42T travel from Taksim.

⛴ **Ferry** Commuter ferries run from Eminönü to Ortaköy in the early evening on weekdays, but there are no return services.

Top Sights
Dolmabahçe Palace

These days it's fashionable for critics influenced by the less-is-more aesthetic of the Bauhaus masters to sneer at buildings such as Dolmabahçe. Enthusiasts of Ottoman architecture also decry this final flourish of the imperial dynasty, dismissing it as vulgarly ostentatious. But whatever the critics might say, this 19th-century palace with its magnificent Bosphorus location, opulent Selâmlık (State or Ceremonial Apartments) and large Harem is a clear crowd favourite.

Dolmabahçe Sarayı

👁 Map p104, A4

www.millisaraylar.gov.tr

Dolmabahçe Caddesi, Beşiktaş

Selâmlık/Harem ₺30/20

🕑9am-6pm Tue-Wed & Fri-Sun

🚇Kabataş, then walk

Don't Miss

Imperial Selâmlık

The palace's state apartments were decorated by Frenchman Charles Séchan, designer of the Paris Opera, and are highly theatrical in appearance. They feature a crystal staircase manufactured by Baccarat, mirrored fireplaces, parquet floors and Sèvres and Yıldız (locally made) porcelain. The most impressive room is the huge Muayede Salon (Ceremonial Hall), which features a purpose-woven 124-sq-metre Hereke carpet and a crystal chandelier weighing 4.5 tonnes.

Imperial Harem

Decoration of the Harem is relatively restrained by Dolmabahçe standards (which, of course, isn't saying much). Its most notable elements are the hand-painted ceilings, which feature throughout. The tour passes bedrooms, private salons (including one decorated with Japanese motifs), a circumcision room and a nursery.

Atatürk's Deathbed

Dolmabahçe was used by the first president of the Republic when he visited İstanbul, and he died here on 10 November 1938. The Harem tour pauses at his bedroom, which features a bed draped in the Turkish flag and a clock stopped at 9.05am, when the great man drew his last breath.

Glass Pavilion

This opulently decorated *köşk* (kiosk) was used by the sultans as a private retreat. Its attached fairytale-like conservatory features etched-glass windows, a crystal fountain and myriad windows. You'll find the kiosk next to the aviary on the street side of the palace.

☑ Top Tips

▶ Visitor numbers in the palace are limited to 3000 per day and this ceiling is often reached on weekends and holidays – come midweek if possible, and even then be prepared to queue (often for a long period and in full sun).

▶ The palace is divided into two sections: the over-the-top Selâmlık and the slightly more restrained Harem. Both are visited on compulsory – and unfortunately rushed – guided tours. If you only take one tour, make it the Selâmlık.

▶ A joint ticket for both the Selâmlık and Harem is available for ₺40.

▶ Opening hours are shorter in winter. See the website for details.

✖ Take a Break

There's a *çay bahçesi* near the clock tower with premium Bosphorus views and bargain prices (yes, really).

Local Life
Weekend Wander in Ortaköy

The settlement of Ortaköy (Turkish for 'Middle Village') dates back to Byzantine times, when it was a small fishing village. These days, the picturesque cobbled laneways surrounding its waterside square, known as İskele (Ferry Dock) Square, are filled with cafes, bars and fast-food stands. On Sundays, a handicrafts market draws visitors from across the city.

① İskele Square

Locals tend to congregate in this attractive square, which fronts the water and has a backdrop of old timber houses now functioning as restaurants and cafes. In its centre is a pretty 18th-century *çeşme* (fountain). On Sundays, the streets surrounding the square are crowded with market stalls selling handicrafts. Cheap imports from the subcontinent and China

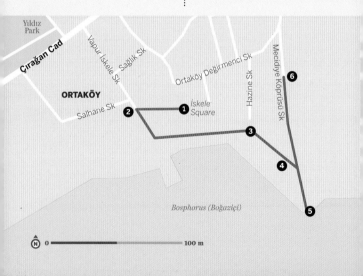

predominate, but some stalls sell handicrafts made by local artisans.

❷ Brunch at the House Cafe

İstanbullus love to brunch, especially if they can do so in glamorous surrounds. The Ortaköy branch of the chic and cheerful **House Cafe** (İskele Meydanı 42; breakfast platters ₺24, sandwiches ₺15-26, pizzas ₺17.50-27.50, mains ₺16.50-29.50; ⏲9am-1am Mon-Thu, to 2am Fri & Sat, to 10.30pm Sun; 🚌Kabataş Lisesi) has a million-lira location right on the water's edge and offers an all-you-can-eat Sunday brunch that is hugely popular with locals.

❸ Sampling Dondurma

Originating in the southeastern region of Maraş, *dondurma* (Turkish ice cream) is made with salep (ground dried orchid root) and mastic (pine-flavoured resin from the mastic tree) as well as milk and sugar. These unusual ingredients give the ice cream a distinctive chewy texture. Sample some at Ortaköy's branch of the **Mado** ice-cream chain, on İskele Sq.

❹ A Perfect Photo Opportunity

With the modern Bosphorus Bridge looming behind it, the 19th-century baroque-style **Ortaköy Mosque**

provides a fabulous photo opportunity for those wanting to illustrate İstanbul's 'old meets new' character. The elegant mosque was designed by Nikoğos Balyan, one of the architects of Dolmabahçe Palace, and built for Sultan Abdül Mecit I between 1853 and 1855. In the light and airy interior, look for several masterful examples of Arabic calligraphy executed by Abdül Mecit, who was an accomplished calligrapher.

❺ Bosphorus Tour

Most tourists jump aboard the crowded excursion ferries at Eminönü to cruise the Bosphorus, but homegrown tourists are more likely to take a one-hour **Bosphorus Tour** (₺10; ⏲weekdays hourly from 2.20pm, weekends every 20min from 1pm) leaving from the ferry dock behind the mosque. These sail to Anadolu Hisarı (Fortress of Asia), the narrowest point of the Bosphorus and back.

❻ Gözleme & Kümpir Stands

The approach to the ferry dock is crowded with stands selling *gözleme* (thin savoury crêpe stuffed with cheese, spinach or potato) or *kümpir* (stuffed baked potato). Either makes a perfect mid-afternoon snack.

500 m
0.25 miles

KURUÇEŞME

Muallim Naci Cad

Bosphorus Bridge
(Boğaziçi Köprüsü)

İskele
Square

Ortaköy
Mosque

Ortaköy Dereboyu Cad

Gültekin Sk

MECİDİYE

Lozan Sk

Çevirmeci Sk

ORTAKÖY

Bosphorus Strait (Boğaziçi)

Fıstıklı Köşk Sk
Saulbaş Sk

Musevi
Mesarlığı

Palanga Cad

Çırağan Cad

Yahya Efendi Sk

To Bosphorus

To Üsküdar

YILDIZ

Yıldız
Park

Çırağan
Palace

Yıldız
Şale

Müvezzi Cad

Asariye Sk

Eski Konak Sk

Çitlenbik Sk

Beşiktaş
Yalı Sk

Yıldız Cad

Serencebey Yokuşu

İhlamur Cad

Barbaros Bul

Eski Yıldız
Cad

Yıldız Posta Cad

İhlamur-Yıldız Cad

To Üsküdar & Bosph

Fulya Deresi Sk

Barış Sk

DİKİLİTAŞ

Çömezler Sk

Abbasağa
Park

Selamlık Cad

Köyiçi Sk

BEŞİKTAŞ

İskele Cad

Odalar Sk

Uzunçova Cad

Dizi Sk

Beşiktaş Cad

Beşiktaş
Cad

Dolmabahçe
Cad

Kadıköy

Mısırlı Bahçe Sk

Hattat Tahsin Sk

Süleyman Seba
(Spor) Cad

Nüzhetiye Cad

Dolmabahçe
Palace

KURUÇEŞME

MECİDİYE

Sights

Yıldız Park

PARK

1 ⊙ Map p104, C2

Abdül Hamit II (r 1876–1909) didn't allow himself to be upstaged by his predecessors, making his architectural mark by adding to the structures built by earlier sultans in Yıldız Park. The pretty *şale* (chalet) that he built here in 1880 originally functioned as a hunting lodge but was converted into a guesthouse for visiting foreign dignitaries in 1889. It's now a museum. (Yıldız Parkı; Çırağan Caddesi, Yıldız; chalet museum adult/child ₺10/5; ⊘chalet museum 9am-4.30pm Tue, Wed & Fri-Sun; 🚌Yahya Efendi)

Çırağan Palace

PALACE

2 ⊙ Map p104, C3

Not satisfied with the architectural exertions of his predecessor at Dolmabahçe, Sultan Abdül Aziz (r 1861–76) built his own grand residence at Çırağan, only 1.5km away. Here, architect Nikoğos Balyan, who had also worked on Dolmabahçe, created an interesting building melding European neoclassical with Ottoman and Moorish styles. The palace is now part of the Çırağan Palace Kempinski Hotel. (Çırağan Sarayı; Çırağan Caddesi 84, Ortaköy; 🚌Çırağan)

Çırağan Palace Kempinski Hotel (p107)

Eating

Sıdıka

TURKISH **$$**

3 🍴 Map p104, A3

Come to this out-of-the-way *meyhane* (tavern) for simply prepared but absolutely sensational fish and vegetable mezes, best sampled in the mixed cold plate (₺30). Follow with some fried fish, a bowl of pasta or – if it's a Friday – a tasty bowl of fish soup. (📞212-259 7232; www.sidika.com.tr; Şair Nedim Caddesi 38 , Beşiktaş; cold mezes ₺3-14, hot mezes ₺15-20, fish ₺16-18; ⊘5pm-midnight Mon-Sat; 🚌Akaretler)

Zuma

JAPANESE $$$

4 Map p104, D2

Good *izakaya*-style food and a stunning waterside location makes the local branch of this London favourite a safe bet. There's a bar and lounge on the top floor and a sushi bar and robata grill downstairs. (☑212-236 2296; www.zumarestaurant.com; Salhane Sokak 7, Ortaköy; veg mains ₺11-26, fish mains ₺28-65, sushi & sashimi ₺39-89; ⊙lunch & dinner; ☑; ☑Kabataş Lisesi)

Vogue

INTERNATIONAL $$$

5 Map p104, A3

It seems as if Vogue has been around for almost as long as the Republic. In fact, this sophisticated bar-restaurant in an office block in Beşiktaş opened just over a decade ago. It's a favourite haunt of local powerbrokers, who tend to enjoy a drink at the terrace bar before moving into the restaurant for dinner. (☑212-227 4404; www.istanbul doors.com; 13th fl, A Blok, BJK Plaza, Spor Caddesi 92, Akaretler; starters ₺25-45, mains ₺28-65; ⊙noon-2am Mon-Sat, 10.30am-2am Sun; ☑; ☑Akaretler)

Banyan

ASIAN $$$

6 Map p104, D2

The menu here travels around Asia, featuring Thai, Japanese, Vietnamese and Chinese dishes including soups, satays and salads. The food is claimed to be good for the soul, and you can enjoy it while revelling in the exceptional views of the Ortaköy Mosque and Bosphorus Bridge from the terrace. (☑212-259 9060; www.banyanrestau rant.com; 3rd fl, Salhane Sokak 3, Ortaköy; starters ₺12-35, mains ₺36-61; ⊙lunch & dinner; ☑Kabataş Lisesi)

Drinking

Reina

CLUB

7 Map p104, E2

According to its website, Reina is where 'foreign heads of states discuss world affairs, business people sign agreements of hundred billions of dollars and world stars visit'. In reality, it's where Turkey's C-list celebrities congregate, the city's nouveaux riches flock and an occasional tourist gets past the doorman to ogle the spectacle and the extraordinary Bosphorus view. (☑212-259 5919; www.reina.com.tr; Muallim Naci Caddesi 44, Ortaköy; cover charge Sat & Sun ₺50, Mon-Fri free; ⊙daily summer, Sat & Sun winter; ☑Ortaköy)

Sortie

CLUB

8 Map p104, E1

Sortie has long vied with Reina as the reigning queen of the Golden Mile, nipping at the heels of its rival dowager. It pulls in the city's glamour-pusses and poseurs, all of whom are on the lookout for the odd celebrity guest. (☑212-327 8585; www.eksenistanbul. com; Muallim Naci Caddesi 141, Kuruçeşme; cover charge Fri & Sat ₺50, Mon-Thu & Sun free; ⊙summer only; ☑Şifa Yurdu)

Anjelique
CLUB

9 Map p104, D2

Occupying a three-storey mansion on the water's edge near İskele Sq, this glam venue is a safe bet if you want to have dinner, a few drinks and a dance or two. Reservations are essential. (☎212-327 2844; www.istanbuldoors.com; Salhane Sokak 10, Ortaköy; no cover charge; ☺6pm-4am; ☒Kabataş Lisesi)

Çırağan Palace
Kempinski Hotel
BAR, CAFE

10 Map p104, C3

Nursing a drink or coffee at one of the Çırağan's terrace tables and watching the scene around the city's most spectacularly sited swimming pool will give you a taste of the lifestyle of the city's rich and famous. (www.ciragan-palace.com; Çırağan Caddesi 32, Ortaköy; ☒Çırağan)

Entertainment

İstanbul Jazz Center
JAZZ

11 Map p104, D2

JC's plays regular host to big names from the international jazz world. You'll need to book in advance (price varies according to the act), and you'll be encouraged to order a fixed menu for dinner (₺60 to ₺70). (☎212-327 5050; www.istanbuljazz.com; Salhane Sokak 10, Ortaköy; ☺from 7pm, live sets 9.30pm & 12.30am Mon-Sat, closed summer; ☒Kabataş Lisesi)

Shopping

Lokum
FOOD

12 Map p104, E1

Lokum (Turkish delight) is elevated to the status of artwork at this boutique in Kuruçeşme. Owner-creator Zeynep Keyman aims to bring back the delights, flavors, knowledge and beauty of Ottoman-Turkish products such as *lokum*, *akide* candies (traditional boiled sweets, sometimes made with nuts and dried fruits), cologne water and scented candles. The gorgeous packaging makes for perfect gifts. (www.lokumistanbul.com; Kuruçeşme Caddesi 19, Kuruçeşme; ☺9am-7pm Mon-Sat; ☒Kuruçeşme)

Haremlique
HOMEWARES

13 Map p104, A3

Come to this shop behind the glamorous W Hotel to source top-drawer bed linen and bathwares. (www.haremlique.com; Şair Nedim Bey Caddesi 11, Beşiktaş; ☺Mon-Sat; ☒Akaretler)

Top Sights
The Bosphorus

Getting There

⚓ **Ferry** The Boğaz Gezileri (Bosphorus Cruise) departs Eminönü daily at 10.35am (one-way/return ₺15/25). Extra service at 1.35pm from April to October; additional noon service in summer.

This mighty strait runs from the Galata Bridge all the way to the Black Sea (Karadeniz), 32km north. Over the centuries it has been crossed by conquering armies, intrepid merchants, fishermen and many an adventurous spirit. To follow in their wake, hop aboard the 90-minute ferry cruise that travels between Eminönü and Anadolu Kavağı, marvelling at the magnificent *yalıs* (waterside timber mansions), ornate Ottoman palaces and massive stone fortresses that line the Asian and European shores (to your right and left, respectively, as you sail down the strait).

Don't Miss

Dolmabahçe & Çırağan Palaces

As the ferry starts its journey from Eminönü, look for the 18th-century tower of **Kız Kulesi** on a tiny island just off the Asian shore. Just before Beşiktaş, on the European shore, you'll pass grandiose **Dolmabahçe Palace** (p100). After a brief stop at Beşiktaş, the ferry passes ornate **Çırağan Palace** (p105), which is now a luxury hotel. Next to it is a long yellow building occupied by Galatasaray University.

Yalıs

Both sides of the Bosphorus shore are lined with *yalıs* built by Ottoman aristocracy and foreign ambassadors in the 17th, 18th and 19th centuries. They are now the most prestigious addresses in town, owned by industrialists, bankers and media tycoons.

Ortaköy Mosque

The dome and two minarets of this 19th-century mosque on the European shore are dwarfed by the adjacent **Bosphorus Bridge**, which was opened in 1973 on the 50th anniversary of the founding of the Turkish Republic.

Beylerbeyi Palace

This 26-room baroque-style **palace** (Beylerbeyi Sarayı; www.millisaraylar.gov.tr; Abdullah Ağa Caddesi, Beylerbeyi; admission ₺20; ☺8.30am-4.30pm Tue, Wed & Fri-Sun; 🚊Beylerbeyi Sarayı) on the Asian shore was built for Abdül Aziz I. Look for its whimsical marble bathing pavilions; one was for men, the other for the women of the Harem.

Bebek

This upmarket suburb is known for its fashion boutiques and chic cafes. As the ferry passes,

☑ Top Tips

▶ If you buy a return ticket you'll have to spend three hours in Anadolu Kavağı (the turnaround point). It's better to buy a one-way ticket and head back to town by bus. This will allow you to stop off and visit sights on your journey back to town. From Anadolu Kavağı, take 15A to Kanlıca, transferring to 15, 15F or 15P for Üsküdar via Küçüksu Kasrı and Beylerbeyi Palace; from Sarıyer, take 25E to Kabataş via Emirgan and Rumeli Hisarı, or 40T to Taksim.

✖ Take a Break

Dine in style on the expansive terrace at **MüzedeChanga** (📞212-323 0901; www.changa-istanbul.com; Sakıp Sabancı Müzesi, Sakıp Sabancı Caddesi 42, Emirgan; starters ₺18-29, mains ₺37-49; ☺10.30am-1am Tue-Sun), overlooking the Bosphorus.

There's a lovely garden cafe at Hıdiv Kasrı (p110).

look for the Ottoman Revivalist–style **Bebek Mosque** and the art nouveau **Egyptian Consulate** building with its mansard roof.

Küçüksu Kasrı

This ornate **hunting lodge** (📞216-332 3303; Küçüksu Caddesi, Beykoz; admission ₺5; ☺9.30am-4pm Tue, Wed & Fri-Sun; 🚇Küçüksu) on the Asian shore was built for Sultan Abdül Mecit from 1856 to 1857. Earlier sultans used wooden kiosks here, but architect Nikoğos Balyan designed a rococo gem in marble for his monarch.

Rumeli Hisarı

Just before the Fatih Bridge is the majestic **Rumeli Hisarı** (Fortress of Europe; 📞212-263 5305; Yahya Kemal Caddesi 42; admission ₺3; ☺9am-noon & 12.30-4.30pm Thu-Tue; 🚇Rumeli Hisarı), built by order of Mehmet the Conqueror in preparation for his siege of Byzantine Constantinople. For its location, he chose the narrowest point of the Bosphorus, opposite **Anadolu Hisarı** (Fortress of Asia), which Sultan Beyazıt I had built in 1391.

Anadolu Hisarı

There are many architecturally and historically important *yalıs* in and around the village of Anadolu Hisarı. These include the **Zarif Mustafa Paşa Yalı**, built in the early 19th century by the official coffee maker to Sultan Mahmud II. Look for its upstairs salon, which juts out over the water and is supported by unusual curved timber struts.

Kanlıca

Past the bridge on the Asian side is Kanlıca, the ferry's second stop. It's famous for the rich and delicious yoghurt produced here, which is sold on the ferry and in two cafes on the shady waterfront square.

Hıdiv Kasrı

High on a promontory above Kanlıca is this gorgeous **art nouveau villa** (Khedive's Villa; www.beltur.com.tr; Çubuklu Yolu 32, Çubuklu; admission free; ☺9am-10pm), built by the last Khedive of Egypt as a summer residence for his family.

Emirgan

On the opposite shore is the wealthy suburb of Emirgan, home to the impressive **Sakıp Sabancı Museum** (Sakıp Sabancı Müzesi; 📞212-277 2200; http://muze.sabanciuniv.edu; Sakıp Sabancı Caddesi 42; exhibition admission varies; ☺10am-6pm Tue, Thu, Fri & Sun, to 10pm Wed & Sat; 🚇Emirgan), which hosts international travelling art exhibitions.

Sarıyer

The ferry's third stop is Sarıyer, on the European shore. Its residents have traditionally made a living by fishing, and the area around the ferry terminal is full of fish restaurants.

Anadolu Kavağı

This village on the Asian shore is the ferry's last stop. Its economy was built on the fishing trade, but these days it relies more on tourism. The main square is full of mediocre fish restaurants.

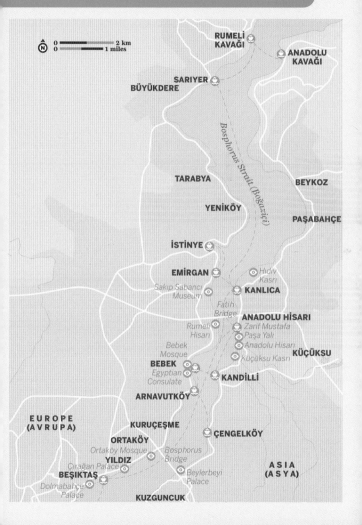

The Best of
İstanbul

Ceiling detail, Blue Mosque (p28)
PETER UNGER/GETTY IMAGES ©

Best Walks
Sultanahmet Saunter

🏃 The Walk

Despite spending the majority of their time in or around Sultanahmet, most visitors see little of this historic district other than their hotel and the major monuments. This walk will take you off the well-worn tourist routes and introduce some lesser-known sights.

Start Sultanahmet Park; 🚃 Sultanahmet

Finish Arasta Bazaar; 🚃 Sultanahmet

Length 2.3km; three hours

✕ Take a Break

There are plenty of tea and coffee options in this area, but few are as atmospheric as the Caferağa Medresesi Lokanta & Çay Bahçesi (p52), set in the tranquil courtyard of the historic *medrese* of the same name.

Fountain of Sultan Ahmet III

❶ Aya Sofya Tombs

Set off from Sultanahmet Park and turn left into Kabasakal Caddesi to visit these splendid Ottoman **tombs** (p33), the final resting places of five sultans.

❷ Fountain of Sultan Ahmet III

This exquisite rococo-style **fountain kiosk** (1728) outside Topkapı Palace once dispensed cold drinks of water and *şerbet* (sweet cordial) to thirsty travellers.

❸ Soğukçeşme Sokak

Veer down this picturesque cobbled **street** (p49), which is home to recreated Ottoman timber houses and a restored Byzantine cistern.

❹ Caferağa Medresesi

Turn left into Caferiye Sokak to visit this lovely little **medrese** (Islamic school of higher studies) tucked away in the shadows of Aya Sofya. Commissioned by Süleyman the Magnificent's chief black eunuch, it was built in 1560 and is now home to an organisation supporting traditional handicrafts.

5 Sokollu Şehit Mehmet Paşa Mosque

Head towards busy Alemdar Caddesi and then veer left to reach the **Hippodrome** (p35). Walk its length and then into Şehit Mehmet Paşa Yokuşu. Continue down Katip Sinan Cami Sokak until you reach this splendid Ottoman-era **mosque**, which has an interior adorned with fine İznik tiles.

6 Little Aya Sofya

Veer left down Şehit Çeşmesı Sokak, then turn left into Kadırga Limanı Caddesi and you'll soon arrive at Küçük Ayasofya Caddesi, home to **Little Aya Sofya** (p35), one of the most beautiful Byzantine buildings in the city.

7 Sphendone

Walk east along Küçük Ayasofya Caddesi and continue left up the hill at Aksakal Caddesi. At the crest is the only remaining built section

of the Hippodrome, the **Sphendone**. Opposite is a huge carpet shop called **Nakkaş** that has a restored Byzantine cistern in its basement.

8 Arasta Bazaar

Continue along Nakilbent Sokak, then veer right down Şifa Hamamı Sokak, turning left into Küçük Ayasofya Caddesi and continuing straight ahead to the **Arasta Bazaar** (p29), a historic row of shops once part of the Blue Mosque *külliye* (mosque complex).

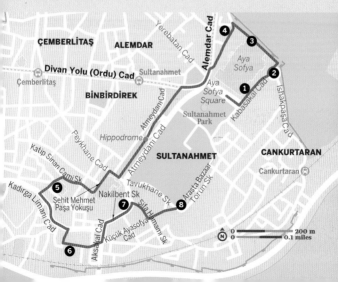

Best Walks
Bohemian Beyoğlu

🏃 The Walk

The streets running off İstiklal Caddesi are the traditional stamping ground of İstanbul's creative communities, and are littered with galleries, artists' ateliers, cafes, bars and boutiques. This walk wends its way through the expat enclave of Cihangir, along the crooked laneways of Çukurcuma and into the music-filled streets of Tünel.

Start Taksim Sq; Ⓜ Taksim

Finish Galata Sq; 🚋 Karaköy

Length 3km; three hours

✗ Take a Break

The neighbourhood of Asmalımescit, west of Tünel, is the hub of Beyoğlu's eating and entertainment scene. On its western (lower) edge is the historic Pera Palace Hotel (p88), where you can enjoy a drink, meal or coffee amid opulent surrounds.

Galata Tower

❶ Taksim Square

Set off from this busy **square** (p79), a popular meeting place for locals.

❷ Cihangir Mosque

From Taksim Sq, walk south down busy Sıraselviler Caddesi and veer left into Arslan Yatağı Sokak. Follow it and Cihangir Caddesi to Susam Sokak, where you should turn right and then almost immediately left to admire a spectacular view of the Old City and Bosphorus from the garden of this **mosque**.

❸ Kardeşler Cafe

Backtrack to Susam Sokak, turn left and follow Şimşirci Sokak into Akarsu Yokuşu. These streets are scattered with local cafes, the most popular of which is this simple place next to the Firuz Ağa Mosque.

❹ Faikpaşa Sokak

Walk past the mosque and turn right into Ağa Hamamı Sokak, passing the historic **hamam** that gives the street its name and then veering left into **Faikpaşa Sokak**, home to alluring antique shops including **A La Turca** (p96).

⑤ Museum of Innocence

Half-way down Faikpaşa Sokak, turn left and then right into Çukurcuma Caddesi. Continue downhill and you'll eventually come to a *çıkmazı* (cul de sac) where Orhan Pamuk's recently opened **Museum of Innocence** (p88) is located.

⑥ ARTER

Backtrack to Çukurcuma Caddesi, turn left and cross busy Yeni Çarşı Caddesi, continuing into Tomtom Kaptan Sk and walking uphill until you reach İstiklal Caddesi. **ARTER** (p79), one of the city's leading contemporary art spaces, is to your left.

⑦ Galata Mevlevi Museum

Continue along İstiklal to Tünel Sq, named after its historic funicular. Turn into Galipdede Caddesi to find the **Galata Mevlevi Museum** (p87), set in a 15th-

century *tekke* (dervish lodge).

⑧ Galata Tower

Continue down Galipdede Caddesi past the shops selling musical instruments to reach the avant-garde district of Galata, home to the landmark **tower** and the subject of our Local Life feature (p82).

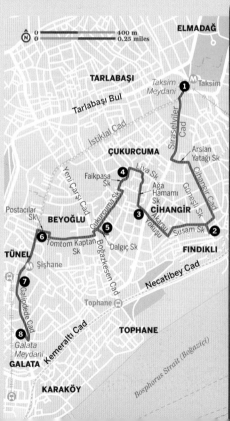

Best
Food

İstanbullus love to eat. Meals are joyful, boisterous and almost inevitably communal. Food is used to celebrate milestones, cement friendships and add cohesion to family life. The idea of eating in front of a TV or out of a freezer is anathema to restaurant chefs and home cooks alike – this is a cuisine that is social, slow and seasonal.

Traditional Eateries

Popular venues for lunch, which is often eaten out, include *lokantas* (eateries serving ready-made food), *pidecis* (Turkish pizza parlours), *kebapçıs* (kebap restaurants) and *köftecis* (meatball restaurants). When not eating dinner at home, locals flock to *meyhanes* (taverns), where an array of hot and cold mezes are served. Fresh fish is enjoyed in *balık restorans* (fish restaurants) and meat in *ocakbaşıs* (fireside kebap restaurants).

Contemporary Cuisine

İstanbul has an ever-growing number of eateries serving Modern Turkish cuisine. Many of these showcase food by chefs who draw inspiration from Turkey's diverse regional cuisines but do so with a European sensibility.

Street Food

Street vendors pound pavements across İstanbul, pushing carts laden with artfully arranged snacks. Look out for *simits* (sesame-encrusted bread rings), *mısır* (corn on the cob), *midye dolma* (stuffed mussels), *çığ köfte* (raw spiced meatballs) and *kokoreç* (skewered lamb or mutton intestines seasoned and grilled over charcoal). The most famous street snack of all is the *balık ekmek* (fish sandwich; see p68).

☑ Top Tips

▶ Popular restaurants are busy on Thursday, Friday and Saturday nights. Book ahead.

▶ Restaurant staff don't always speak English – ask staff at your hotel to make your booking.

▶ Alcohol is served in most restaurants reviewed in this book. Exceptions are noted.

Best Meyhanes

Asmalı Cavit Old-fashioned ambience and the best *meyhane* food in the city. (p88)

Sofyalı 9 Bustling atmosphere and a wide array of mezes. (p90)

Mezes

Sıdıka Sensational fish mezes. (p105)

Karaköy Lokantası Charming decor and good food. (p89)

Demeti Neighbourhood eatery serving Mediterranean-style mezes. (p92)

Jash Armenian specialities and live music. (p92)

Best Kebaps

Zübeyir Ocakbaşı Succulent meats cooked over coals. (p89)

Hamdi Restaurant Specialities from Turkey's southeast, plus an amazing view. (p67)

Best Modern Turkish

Lokanta Maya Stylish bistro serving modern takes on traditional dishes. (p88)

Meze by Lemon Tree Elegant surrounds, delectable food and a good wine list. (p89)

MüzedeChanga Sophisticated lunch venue on the Bosphorus. (p109)

Mikla Fine dining, luxe surrounds and spectacular views. (p91)

Changa Pioneered fusion in the city. (p90)

Best Ottoman Cuisine

Asitane Decadent dishes once served to the sultans. (p75)

Matbah Palace cuisine in a garden setting. (p51)

Cihannüma Extraordinary views and tasty dishes. (p51)

Best Snacks

Dönerci Şahin Usta The best döner kebap in the Old City. (p63)

Fatih Damak Pide Wonderful neighbourhood *pideci*. (p67)

Asmalı Canım Ciğerim Liver kebaps beloved of aficionados. (p91)

Best Sweets

Karaköy Güllüoğlu The perfect baklava stop at any time of day. (p88)

Hafız Mustafa Offers a huge array of sweet temptations. (p51)

Best Drinking

İstanbul may be the biggest city in a predominantly Muslim country, but İstanbullus like nothing more than a drink or two. To join them, head to the bars and taverns in Beyoğlu and along the Bosphorus. On the Historical Peninsula, the tipples of choice are çay (tea) or *türk kahve* (Turkish coffee).

Rakı

Turkey's most beloved tipple is rakı, a grape spirit infused with aniseed. Similar to Greek ouzo, it's served in long thin glasses and drunk neat or with water, which turns the clear liquid chalky white.

Turkish Wine

Turkey grows and bottles its own *şarap* (wine), which is extremely quaffable but expensive due to high government taxes. If you want red wine, ask for *kırmızı şarap*; for white wine, *beyaz şarap*. As well as producing vintages of well-known grape varieties, Turkish winemakers also use local varietals including *boğazkere* and *buzbağ* (strong-bodied reds), *emir* (a light and floral white), *kalecik karası* (an elegant red) and *narince* (a fruity yet dry white).

Turkish Coffee

A thick and powerful brew, *türk kahve* is drunk in a couple of short sips. If you order a cup, you will be asked how sweet you like it – *çok şekerli* means 'very sweet', *orta şekerli* 'middling', *az şekerli* 'slightly sweet' and *şekersiz* or *sade* 'not at all'.

Turkish Tea

Drinking çay is the national pastime. Sugar cubes are the only accompaniment: you'll find you need these to counter the effects of long brewing, or you can always try asking for it *açık* (weaker).

PHOTO: GÜL KAPLAN/GETTY IMAGES ©

☑ Top Tips

▶ Coffee aficionados should head to Müzenin Kahvesi, the stylish cafe-laboratory in the courtyard of the Museum of Turkish & Islamic Arts (p35), to take its 30-minute 'Treasures of Turkey' coffee experience (₺20). This demonstrates roasting, grinding, brewing and service techniques and includes – naturally – a cup of the stuff in question. Bookings essential.

Leb-i Derya (p93)

Best Rooftop Bars

Mikla Spectacular views and a stylish clientele. (p92)

360 The city's most famous bar for good reason. (p93)

NuTeras Golden Horn (Haliç) views and a chic after-dinner club scene. (p94)

Leb-i Derya Bosphorus views and a down-to-earth crowd. (p93)

X Bar A seductive mix of culture and cocktails. (p94)

Ca' d'Oro Crowning glory of the cutting-edge SALT Cultural Centre. (p89)

Best Turkish Coffee

Manda Batmaz Traditional coffeehouse in Beyoğlu. (p92)

Müzenin Kahvesi Set in the courtyard of the Museum of Turkish & Islamic Arts. (p35)

Fes Cafe Great coffee with a *lokum* (Turkish delight) chaser. (p68)

Best Boutique Bars

Baylo Elegant surrounds and an arty vibe. (p94)

Münferit Where the in-crowd enjoys its aperitifs. (p93)

Le Fumoir Chic bar-restaurant in Galata's most atmospheric street. (p83)

Best
Architecture

İstanbul is one of the world's great architectural time capsules. Here, locals live within city walls built by Byzantine emperors, worship in Ottoman-era mosques and reside in grand 19th-century apartment buildings.

Byzantine Architecture

The city spent 1123 years as a Christian metropolis and many structures survive from this era. After the Conquest, numerous churches were converted into mosques; despite the minarets, you can usually tell a church-cum-mosque by its distinctive red bricks. The Byzantines also built aqueducts, cisterns and public squares that exist to this day.

Ottoman Architecture

After the Conquest, the sultans made their mark by constructing mosques, palaces, hamams, *medreses* and *yalıs* (waterside timber mansions). The greatest of these were commissioned by Süleyman the Magnificent and designed by his court architect, Mimar Sinan. Later sultans focused on palaces and hunting lodges featuring ornate external detailing and ostentatious interior decoration; these and other buildings of the era have been collectively dubbed 'Turkish baroque'.

Ottoman Revivalism & Modernism

In the late 19th century, architects blended European architecture with Turkish baroque, along with some concessions to classic Ottoman style. This style has been dubbed 'Ottoman Revivalism' or First National Architecture. When the 20th century arrived and Atatürk proclaimed Ankara the capital of the republic, İstanbul lost much of its glamour and investment capital.

☑ **Top Tips**

▶ Architectural walking tours of the city are conducted by İstanbul Walks (www.istanbulwalks.net), a company run by a group of history, conservation and architecture buffs. Tours run daily and can be booked at short notice.

Best Byzantine Buildings

Aya Sofya One of the world's great buildings, with a magnificent interior. (p24)

Little Aya Sofya An exquisite church building sympathetically converted into a mosque. (p35)

Basilica Cistern Extraordinary engineering and

Çırağan Palace (p105)

a stunning symmetrical design. (p30)

Rumeli Hisarı A massive structure strategically located on the narrowest point of the Bosphorus. (p110)

Best Ottoman Buildings

Topkapı Palace Pavilion-style architecture and a gorgeous landscaped setting. (p42)

Süleymaniye Mosque The greatest of the city's imperial mosques, with many intact outbuildings. (p60)

Blue Mosque A profusion of minarets, domes and fine İznik tilework. (p28)

Ayasofya Hürrem Sultan Hamamı Elegant twin hamam built for a sultan's wife. (p124)

Best Turkish Baroque Buildings

Dolmabahçe Palace Imposing exterior and over-the-top interior decoration. (p100)

Beylerbeyi Palace Imperial splendour on the Asian shore of the Bosphorus. (p109)

Çırağan Palace Little sister to Dolmabahçe, with a similar design and location. (p105)

Küçüksu Kasrı Ornately designed imperial retreat built on the Bosphorus shore. (p110)

Best Contemporary Adaptive Reuse

SALT Galata 1892 bank building cleverly converted into gallery, library and restaurant spaces. (p83)

İstanbul Modern A shipping warehouse converted into a huge contemporary art gallery. (p80)

SALT Beyoğlu 1850s apartment block converted into a multilevel cultural centre. (p79)

Sakıp Sabancı Museum Sympathetic modern additions to one of the largest mansions on the Bosphorus. (p110)

Best
Hamams

Succumbing to a soapy scrub in a traditional hamam is one of the city's quintessential experiences. Not everyone feels comfortable with baring their body in public, though. In these cases, a private hamam treatment in one of the city's spas is a good alternative.

Bath Procedure

Upon entry you will be shown to a *camekan* (entrance hall), allocated a dressing cubicle and given a *peştemal* (bath wrap) and plastic sandals. Undress and put these on. Females may keep a bikini bottom or pair of knickers on, although this is optional. Males usually just wear the *peştemal* (but always leave it on). You'll then be shown to the *hararet* (steam room), where you can sit on the side or lie on top of the central *göbektaşı* (heated raised platform).

The cheapest option is to bring your own soap, shampoo and towel and wash yourself. But the real Turkish bath experience involves having an attendant wash, scrub and massage you. Soap, shampoo and towel are included in these treatments; you may wish to bring your own *kese* (exfoliating mitten).

Ayasofya Hürrem Sultan Hamamı (☑212-517 3535; www.ayasofyahamami. com; Aya Sofya Meydanı; bath treatments €70-165, massages €40-75; ◷8am-11pm; ☐Sultanahmet) This meticulously restored twin hamam dates from 1556 and offers the most luxurious traditional bath experience in the Old City.

Çemberlitaş Hamamı (☑212-522 7974; Vezir Han Caddesi 8; bath, scrub & soap massage €29; ◷6am-midnight; ☐Çemberlitaş) Another gorgeous Ottoman twin hamam (dating from 1584).

Four Seasons Istanbul at the Bosphorus (☑212-381 4160; www.fourseasons. com/bosphorus; Çırağan Caddesi 28; Beşiktaş; massage €140-250, 30/45min hamam experience €100/150; ◷9am-9pm; ☐Bahçeşehir Unv or Çırağan) This luxury hotel spa is the perfect choice if you're looking for an indulgent Turkish bath experience.

Cağaloğlu Hamamı (☑212-522 2424; www.caga logluhamami.com.tr; Yerebatan Caddesi 34; bath, scrub & massage packages €50-110; ◷8am-10pm; ☐Sultanahmet) Built in 1741 by order of Sultan Mahmut I, this twin hamam has a magnificent interior.

Best
Nargile Cafes

stanbullus have perfected the art of *keyif* (quiet relaxation), and practise it at every possible opportunity. Nargile (water pipe) cafes are *keyif* central, offering their patrons pockets of tranquility off the noisy and crowded streets. Games of *tavla* (backgammon), glasses of tea, nargiles and quiet conversations are usually the only distractions on offer.

Ordering a Nargile

You'll need to specify what type of tobacco you would like. Most people opt for *elma* (when the tobacco has been soaked in apple juice, giving it a sweet flavour and scent), but it's possible to order it unadulterated *(tömbeki)* or in a variety of other fruit flavours. A nargile usually costs between ₺15 and ₺25 and can be shared (you'll be given individual plastic mouthpieces).

Accompaniments

Locals usually drink çay when they are enjoying a nargile, beckoning the waiter over for regular refills. At the nargile cafes in Tophane, plates of fresh fruit and nuts are set up on each table – you'll pay for what you eat. Other snacks can be ordered with the waiter.

Türk Ocaği Kültür ve Sanat Merkezi İktisadi İşletmesi Çay Bahçesi In an Ottoman cemetery on Divan Yolu. (p38)

Yeni Marmara Authentic and atmospheric neighbourhood cafe. (p38)

Best Beyoğlu Nargile Cafes

Tophane Nargile Cafes A cluster of *çay bahcesis* (tea gardens) behind the Nusretiye Mosque in Tophane. (p92)

Best Old City Nargile Cafes

Erenler Çay Bahçesi Set in the vine-covered courtyard of the Çorlulu Ali Paşa Medrese near the Grand Bazaar. (p69)

Lale Bahçesi Located in a sunken courtyard in the shadow of the Süleymaniye Mosque. (p69)

Derviş Aile Çay Bahçesi A leafy retreat opposite the Blue Mosque. (p37)

ROAD TRIPPIN'/ALAMY ©

Best
Museums &
Galleries

İstanbul has always embraced art and culture. In Byzantine times, the emperors amassed huge collections of antiquities, importing precious items from every corner of their empire. The Ottoman sultans followed the same tradition, building extraordinary imperial collections. And these days, the country's big banks and business dynasties vie to outdo each other in building and endowing galleries and cultural centres.

Best Museums

İstanbul Archaeology Museums An extraordinary collection of antiquities, classical sculpture, historical artefacts and Ottoman tilework. (p46)

Museum of Turkish & Islamic Arts The world's best collection of Oriental carpets. (p35)

Great Palace Mosaic Museum Showcases a stunning mosaic pavement dating from Byzantine times. (p33)

Best Art Galleries

İstanbul Modern Spotlights 20th-century Turkish painting alongside high-profile international artists. (p80)

ARTER Four floors of cutting-edge contemporary art on İstiklal Caddesi. (p79)

Pera Museum Turkey's most significant collection of Orientalist paintings. (p87)

SALT Beyoğlu Cultural centre with an emphasis on video and installation arts. (p79)

☑ **Top Tips**

▶ If you plan on visiting the major museums and monuments, the Museum Pass İstanbul (www.muze.gov.tr/museum_pass) will save you money and time. See p140 for details.

SALT Galata Visual arts exhibitions, lectures and performances. (p83)

Sakıp Sabancı Museum Hosts top-notch travelling international art exhibitions. (p110)

Best
Views

Istanbul has one of the world's greatest skylines, studded with historic minarets, domes and towers. The hilly topography is fringed with waterways (the Bosphorus, Golden Horn and Sea of Marmara) and retains a surprisingly generous allocation of green spaces, including heavily treed parks and garden cemeteries. Together, these attributes offer views that are guaranteed to delight.

Scenic Viewpoints

The city's many hills are invariably crowned with Ottoman mosques, most of which incorporate scenic terraces. And these weren't the only Ottoman buildings that were designed to make the most of their location – imperial palaces and pleasure kiosks were almost always sited to take advantage of spectacular water vistas.

Rooftop Bars & Cafes

One of the most delightful experiences on offer is to enjoy a drink or meal in a rooftop cafe, bar or restaurant. Occupying the top floors of hotels and commercial buildings in Sultanahmet, Beyoğlu and along the Bosphorus shore, these venues give the city's eating and drinking scenes a unique allure. See p121 for our list of best rooftop bars.

Best Views from Monuments

Topkapı Palace Marble Terrace and Treasury Terrace. (p42)

Rumeli Hisarı Extraordinary Bosphorus views from the ramparts. (p110)

Dolmabahçe Palace The Bosphorus location ensures spectacular views. (p100)

Süleymaniye Mosque Golden Horn vistas from the terrace behind the mosque. (p60)

Cihangir Mosque Panoramic view of the Old City and Bosphorus from the mosque's garden. (p116)

Best Restaurant Views

Cihannüma The best view in the Old City. (p51)

Hamdi Restaurant Amazing Bosphorus, Golden Horn and Old City views. (p67)

Ca' d'Oro Expansive view of the Old City, Bosphorus and Golden Horn. (p89)

Mikla Spectacular 360-degree views across the city. (p91)

Vogue Across the Bosphorus to the Old City and Asian shore. (p106)

Best
Shopping

Over centuries, İstanbullus have perfected the practice of shopping. Trading is in their blood and they've turned making a sale or purchase into an art form. Go into any carpet shop and you'll see what we mean – there's etiquette to be followed, tea to be drunk, conversation to be had. And, of course, there's money to be spent and made.

Bathwares

Towels, *peştemals* and bathrobes made on hand looms in southern Turkey are popular purchases, as are olive-oil soaps and hamam sets (soap, exfoliation glove and hamam bowl).

Carpets & Kilims

The carpet industry is rife with commissions, fakes and dodgy merchandise, so you need to be extremely wary in all of your dealings.

Textiles

Turkey's southeast is known for its textiles, and there are examples aplenty on show in the Grand Bazaar. Also look for decorative tribal textiles that have made their way here from Central Asia. These are often sold in carpet shops.

Ceramics

Many of the Turkish tiles and plates you see in the tourist shops have been painted using a silkscreen printing method and this is why they're cheap. Hand-painted pieces are more expensive.

Jewellery

Look for work by the city's growing number of artisans making contemporary pieces inspired by local culture.

☑ Top Tips

▶ *Lokum* (Turkish delight) makes a great present for those at home. It's sold in speciality shops around the city.

Best Homewares

Dear East Designer homewares made by local and international artisans. (p83)

Haremlique Top-drawer bathwares and bed linen. (p107)

Tulu Cushions, bedding and accessories inspired by textiles from Central Asia. (p39)

İroni Silver-plated tea sets and light fittings referencing traditional Turkish designs. (p83)

Ceramics displayed at the Grand Bazaar (p56)

Best Bathwares

Jennifer's Hamam Bath linens produced on old-style hand looms. (p38)

Abdulla Natural Products Stylish bath linens and pure olive-oil soap. (p70)

Derviş *Peştemals*, hamam bowls and felt-work. (p70)

Hammam Naturally scented soaps. (p97)

Best Carpets & Kilims

Cocoon Textiles, rugs and handicrafts from Central Asia. (p38)

Mehmet Çetinkaya Gallery Heirloom rugs and textiles. (p38)

Dhoku Kilims featuring contemporary designs. (p72)

A La Turca Atmospheric Beyoğlu store full of antique kilims. (p96)

Best Jewellery

Sevan Bıçakçı Contemporary pieces inspired by the monuments and history of İstanbul. (p73)

Selda Okutan Sculptural pieces featuring tiny naked figures. (p97)

Serhat Geridönmez Copies of Hellenistic, Roman and Byzantine jewellery. (p72)

Best Textiles

Muhlis Günbattı Fine cotton bedspreads and tablecloths embroidered with silk. (p72)

Yazmacı Necdet Danış Famous Grand Bazaar fabric store. (p72)

Best Handicrafts

Ak Gümüş Central Asian tribal arts. (p72)

Beyoğlu Olgunlaşma Enstitüsü Beyoğlu retail outlet of local handicrafts school. (p96)

Lâl Accessories and T-shirts made by traditional artisans but featuring a contemporary design aesthetic. (p83)

Best Turkish Delight

Lokum Boutique shop known for its exquisite packaging. (p107)

Ali Muhiddin Hacı Bekir The city's most famous outlet, with branches in Eminönü and Beyoğlu. (p53)

Best
Nightlife

There's a nightlife option for everyone in İstanbul. You can while away the night in a glamorous nightclub on the Bosphorus, listen to bands in a grungy Beyoğlu venue or drink rakı and burst into song at a cheap and rowdy *meyhane* or *Türkü evi* (Turkish music bar).

Clubs

The best nightclubs are in Beyoğlu and on the Golden Mile between Ortaköy and Kuruçeşme on the Bosphorus. Friday and Saturday are the busiest nights of the week and action rarely kicks off before 1am. Note that many of the Beyoğlu clubs close over summer, when clubbing action moves to coastal resorts south of the city or to the Golden Mile. Most of the Bosphorus clubs close over winter.

Live-Music Venues

Beyoğlu is the heart of the city's live-music scene, and clubs such as Babylon regularly program performances by live bands (see p96). But for a uniquely Turkish experience you should consider visiting a *Türkü evi*, where live *halk meziği* (folk music) is performed.

Meyhanes

On weekends, locals like to get together with friends and family at *meyhanes*. Some *meyhanes* focus solely on food, but others host small groups of musicians who move from table to table playing *fasıl* music, emotion-charged Turkish folk or pop songs played on traditional instruments. These are favourites with large groups, who pay a set charge of between ₺70 and ₺100 to enjoy a generous set menu with either limited or unlimited choices from the bar.

☑ **Top Tips**

▶ If you're keen to visit a Bosphorus club, consider booking to have dinner in its restaurant – otherwise you could be looking for a lucky break or be up for a tip of at least ₺100 to get past the door staff.

▶ When İstanbullus go out clubbing they dress to kill. You'll need to do the same to get past the door staff at the Bosphorus clubs or into the rooftop bar-clubs in Beyoğlu.

Reina (p106)

Best Clubs

Babylon The best live-music venue in town. (p95)

MiniMüzikHol Hub of the avant-garde arts scene. (p93)

Dogzstar Bands, DJs and an outdoor terrace. (p94)

Reina Queen of the Golden Mile superclubs. (p106)

Sortie Bosphorus views and celebrity clientele. (p106)

Best Gay & Lesbian Venues

Love Dance Point Inclusive crowd and eclectic playlist.

Tek Yön Cruisers and cuddly bears take to the huge dance floor. (p95)

Bigudi Cafe The city's most accessible lesbian venue. (p94)

Club 17 An exhilarating crush on the weekend; more bar than club. (p94)

Worth a Trip

Going into its second decade, **Love Dance Point** (www.lovedp.net; Cumhuriyet Caddesi 349, Harbiye; 11.30pm-5am Fri & Sat) is easily the most Europhile of the local gay venues, hosting musical icons and international circuit parties. Hard-cutting techno is thrown in with gay anthems and Turkish pop, attracting a varied clientele. You'll find it in the suburb of Harbiye, a short walk from Taksim Sq.

Best For Kids

If you're after a family-friendly city break, İstanbul is the perfect choice. Your children might whinge about the number of mosques and museums on the daily itinerary, but they'll be quickly appeased by the fantastic baklava, *lokum* (Turkish delight) and *dondurma* (ice cream; pictured right) to be sampled, not to mention the castles, underground cisterns and parks to be explored.

Best for Toddlers

Gülhane Park Playground equipment and plenty of open space. (p49)

Hippodrome More open space to run around in. (p35)

Best for Bigger Kids

Bosphorus Cruise Spot monuments from both sides of the boat. (p108)

Rumeli Hisarı Kids love castles! Just be careful that junior knights and princesses don't go too close to the edge on the battlements. (p110)

Basilica Cistern It's creepy (way cool), and kids can explore the walkways suspended over the water. (p30)

Hafız Mustafa Cakes, pastries and ice cream. Yum. (p51)

Best for Teenagers

İstanbul Modern Plenty of exhibits – including lots of multimedia – that will amuse and engage. (p80)

☑ Top Tips

▶ Kids under 12 receive free or discounted entry to most museums and monuments.

▶ Kids under seven travel free on public transport.

▶ Most pavements are cobbled, so strollers aren't very useful – bring a backpack carrier instead.

Survival Guide

Survival Guide

Before You Go

When to Go

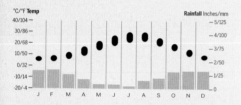

°C/°F Temp
Rainfall Inches/mm

→ Spring (Mar-May)
Possibly the best time of the year to visit; tulips bloom in April.

→ Summer (Jun-Aug)
The heat can seem unrelenting, but discounted hotel rates and the İstanbul Music Festival compensate.

→ Autumn (Sep-Nov)
A lovely time of year, with gentle breezes and a profusion of cultural festivals.

→ Winter (Dec-Feb)
Winters are often bone-chillingly cold. Low-season rates apply in hotels except over the Christmas/New Year period.

Book Your Stay

→ Staying in Sultanahmet makes sense if you plan to spend most of your time visiting museums and the bazaars. Beyoğlu is a better option for those interested in eating, drinking and clubbing.

→ Book your room as far in advance as possible, particularly if you are visiting during the high season (Easter to May, September, October and Christmas/New Year).

→ Check out lonelyplanet. com for accommodation recommendations and bookings.

→ Many hotels offer a discount of between 5% and 10% for cash payments. Room rates in the low season (November to Easter, excluding Christmas/New Year) and shoulder season (June to August) are often discounted.

→ A Value-Added Tax (VAT) of 8% is added to all hotel

ills; it's usually included n the price quoted when ou book.

◆ Most hotels provide a ree airport transfer from Atatürk International Airport if you stay three ights or more.

Breakfast is almost always included in the oom rate.

◆ Rental apartments are rarely in blocks with elevators – be prepared or stairs if you've booked something with a view.

Best Budget

Hanedan Hotel (www. hanedanhotel.com) Cheap, clean and comfortable.

Marmara Guesthouse (www.marmaraguesthouse.com) Friendly, family-run choice.

Hotel Peninsula (www. hotelpeninsula.com) Comfortable rooms and a welcoming atmosphere.

Hotel Alp (www. alpguesthouse.com) Budget prices but midrange facilities, including a wonderful roof terrace.

Best Midrange

Hotel İbrahim Paşa (www.ibrahimpasha.com) Exemplary boutique hotel with wonderful roof terrace.

Sirkeci Konak (www. sirkecikonak.com) Fantastic service, facilities and entertainment program.

Sarı Konak Hotel (www. istanbulhotelsarikonak. com) Classy choice with good amenities.

Hotel Empress Zoe (www.emzoe.com) Boutique choice with wonderful garden suites.

Acra Hotel (www.acra hotel.com) Large, extremely comfortable rooms and a breakfast space incorporating Byzantine features.

Anemon Galata (www. anemonhotels.com) Elegant decor, a wine bar and a roof terrace with sensational views.

Best Top End

Four Seasons Istanbul at the Bosphorus (www. fourseasons.com/bosphorus) The city's best

hotel, with a simply extraordinary pool terrace.

Tom Tom Suites (www. tomtomsuites.com) Elegant suite rooms and a rooftop restaurant with spectacular views.

Sumahan on the Water (www.sumahan.com) Understated luxury on the Bosphorus, complete with a private motor launch.

Ajia (www.ajiahotel. com) Hip ambience and a Bosphorus location that's perfect for a romantic retreat.

Best Suite Hotels

Beş Oda (www.5oda. com) Designer choice in a fantastic location.

Galateia Residence (www.galateiaresidence. com) Luxury apartments perfect for businesspeople.

Witt Istanbul Hotel (www.wittistanbul.com) Stylish choice in a great neighbourhood.

Serdar-ı Ekrem 59 (www.serdar-iekrem59. com) Old-world charm melds with modern amenities.

Arriving in İstanbul

☑ **Top Tip** For the best way to get to your accommodation, see p17.

Atatürk International Airport

➡ Lies 23km west of Sultanahmet; the *dış hatlar* (international terminal) and *iç hatlar* (domestic terminal) are side by side.

➡ A **taxi** costs around ₺40 from the airport to Sultanahmet, ₺50 to Taksim Sq.

➡ An efficient **metro** service (₺2) travels between the airport and Zeytinburnu, from where it's easy to connect with the **tram** (₺2) to Sultanahmet, Eminönü and Kabataş. From Kabataş, there's a **funicular** (₺2) to Taksim Sq. The metro station is on the lower ground floor beneath the international departures hall – follow the 'Metro/Subway' signs down the escalators and through the underground walkway. Services depart every 10 minutes or so from 5.40am until 1.40am. The entire trip takes approximately 60 minutes to Sultanahmet,

70 minutes to Eminönü and 95 minutes to Taksim.

➡ If you're staying in Beyoğlu, take the **Havataş Airport Bus** (₺10). This travels between the arrivals hall and Cumhuriyet Caddesi, next to Taksim Sq, every 30 minutes between 4am and 1am; the trip takes between 40 minutes and one hour, depending on traffic.

Sabiha Gökçen International Airport

➡ Lies 50km east of Sultanahmet, on the Asian side of the city, and is popular with cut-price European carriers.

➡ A **taxi** costs around ₺120 from the airport to Sultanahmet, ₺90 to Taksim Sq.

➡ The **Havataş Airport Bus** (₺12) travels from the airport to Taksim Sq in Beyoğlu between 5am and midnight; after midnight there are shuttle services 30 minutes after every flight arrival. The trip takes approximately 90 minutes. If you're heading towards Sultanahmet, you'll then need to take the **funicular** (₺2) to Kabataş and the **tram** (₺2) from Kabataş.

Getting Around

Tram

☑ **Best for...** Travelling between Sultanahmet and Beyoğlu.

➡ An excellent *tramvay* (tramway) service runs from Bağcılar, in the city's west, to Zeytinburnu (where it connects with the metro from the airport) and on to Sultanahmet and Eminönü. It then crosses the Galata Bridge to Karaköy (to connect with the Tünel) and Kabataş (to connect with the funicular to Taksim Sq).

➡ Services run every five minutes from 6am to midnight.

➡ The fare is ₺2; *jetons* (transport tokens) are available from machines on every tram stop.

Funicular

☑ **Best for...** The steep uphill climb from all tram stops to İstiklal Caddesi.

➡ A funicular saves passengers the steep walk from Karaköy to İstiklal Caddesi. Known as the Tünel, the three-minute service (₺1.40) operates every five or 10 minutes

Tickets & Passes

If you plan to use public transport during your time in the city, consider purchasing an **İstanbulkart**. These rechargeable travel cards are simple to operate: as you enter a bus or pass through the turnstile at a ferry dock, tram stop or metro station, swipe your card for entry and the fare will automatically be deducted from your balance. The cards offer a considerable discount on fares and they can be used to pay for fares for more than one traveller (one swipe per person per ride).

The cards can be purchased for a refundable deposit of ₺10 and charged with amounts between ₺5 and ₺150. Unfortunately, they are a bit difficult to access – you need to find a kiosk displaying an 'Akbil' or 'İstanbulkart' sign. The most conveniently located kiosk for travellers is at the bus station at Eminönü. Cards can be recharged at machines or kiosks at ferry docks, metro stations and bus stations.

...rom 7am to 9pm Monday to Friday (from 7.30am on weekends).

...` Another funicular connects the Kabataş tram stop with the metro station at Taksim Sq. The service operates between 6am to midnight and *Jetons* cost ₺2.

Ferry

☑ **Best for...** Sightseeing and travelling on the Bosphorus and Golden Horn (Haliç).

→ The main ferry docks are at the mouth of the Golden Horn (Eminönü and Karaköy) and at Beşiktaş, a few kilometres northeast of Galata Bridge, near Dolmabahçe Palace. There are also busy docks at Kadıköy and Üsküdar on the Asian (Anatolian) side. The following routes are commonly used by travellers:

Eminönü–Anadolu Kavağı Take the Boğaz Gezileri (Bosphorus Cruise); between one and three services per day.

Eminönü–Kadıköy Approximately every 15 to 20 minutes from 7.30am to 9.10pm.

Eminönü–Üsküdar Approximately every 20 minutes from 6.35am to 11pm.

Karaköy–Kadıköy Approximately every 20 minutes from 6.10am to 11pm.

Üsküdar–Eminönü– Kasımpaşa–Hasköy– Ayvansaray–Sütlüce– Eyüp The Golden Horn (Haliç) ferry; approximately every hour from 10.45am to 8pm, earlier on weekdays.

→ *Jetons* cost ₺2 for most trips and it's possible to use İstanbulkarts on all routes. **İstanbul Şehir Hatları** (İstanbul City Routes; www.sehirhatlari.com. tr) has fare and timetable information.

→ Private Bosphorus excursion boats (₺10) depart Eminönü regularly, travelling as far as Anadolu Hisarı and back without stopping.

Taxi

☑ **Best for...** Travelling at night or if you are short on time.

→ Taxi rates are very reasonable (the trip from

Sultanahmet to Taksim Sq will cost around ₺15) and there are no evening surcharges.

➡ Ignore taxi drivers who insist on a fixed rate as these are much higher than you'd pay using the meter.

➡ Note that few of the city's taxis have seatbelts.

➡ If you take a taxi over either of the Bosphorus bridges, it's your responsibility to cover the toll. The driver will add this to the fare.

Metro

☑ **Best for...** Trips to the airport.

➡ One service connects Aksaray with the airport, stopping at 15 stations on the way. Services depart every 10 minutes or so from 5.40am until 1.40am and a *jeton* costs ₺2.

➡ Another service connects Şişhane, near Tünel Sq in Beyoğlu, with Taksim Sq at the opposite end of İstiklal Caddesi. From Taksim Sq, a line travels to business and residential suburbs northeast. Services run every five minutes or so from 6.15am to midnight. *Jetons* cost ₺2.

➡ Works are currently underway to extend the Taksim–Şişhane route over the Golden Horn via a new metro bridge and under the Old City to Yenikapı via stops at Unkapanı and Şehzadebaşı. It will then connect with the metro to Aksaray and with a transport tunnel being built under the Bosphorus as part of the city's huge Marmaray transport project.

Bus

☑ **Best for...** Exploring the Bosphorus villages.

➡ The major *otobus* (bus) stations are at Taksim Sq, Beşiktaş, Eminönü, Kadıköy and Üsküdar.

➡ Most services run between 6.30am and 11.30pm.

➡ You'll need to purchase a ticket (₺2) before boarding. Buy these from the white booths near major stops or from some nearby shops for a small mark-up (look for 'İETT otobüs bileti satılır' signs). Better still, use an İstanbulkart.

➡ For bus timetables and route details, see the website of the **İstanbul Elektrik Tramvay ve Tünel** (İETT, Istanbul Electricity, Tramway & Tunnel General Management; www.iett.gov.tr).

Essential Information

Business Hours

☑ **Top Tip** Final entry to most museums is generally an hour before the official closing time. We have cited the closing time in our reviews.

Opening hours vary wildly across businesses

Opening Hours

BUSINESS	HOURS
Post offices & banks	8.30am–noon & 1.30-5.30pm Mon-Fri
Shops	9am-7pm Mon-Sat
Restaurants & cafes	breakfast 7.30-10.30am, lunch noon-2.30pm, dinner 7.30-10pm
Bars	afternoon to early morning
Nightclubs	10pm till late

and services in İstanbul. See the boxed text for a general guide.

Electricity

230V/50Hz

Emergency

Ambulance (☎112)

Fire (☎110)

Police (☎155)

Tourist Police (☎212-527 4503; Yerebatan Caddesi 6)

Money

➜ The currency is the Türk Lirası (Turkish Lira; ₺).

➜ ATMS are widely available.

➜ Most hotels, car-rental agencies, shops, pharmacies, entertainment

venues and restaurants accept Visa and Master-Card; Amex isn't as widely accepted and Diners is often not accepted. Inexpensive eateries usually accept cash only.

➜ The 24-hour *döviz bürosu* (exchange bureaux) in the arrivals halls of the international airports usually offer competitive rates.

➜ Tip 10% in restaurants and ₺2 per bag for bellboys; in taxis round up the fare to the nearest ₺1.

Public Holidays

New Year's Day 1 January

National Sovereignty & Children's Day 23 April

May Day 1 May

Atatürk Commemoration & Youth Day 19 May

Victory Day 30 August

Republic Day 29 October

Religious festivals are celebrated according to the Muslim lunar Hejira calendar; two of these festivals (Şeker Bayramı and Kurban Bayramı) are also public holidays. Şeker Bayramı is a three-day festival at the end of Ramazan, and Kurban Bayramı, the most important religious holiday of the year, is a four-day festival whose dates change each year. During these festivals, banks and offices are closed and hotels, buses, trains and planes are heavily booked.

Safe Travel

➜ Theft is not generally a big problem and robbery (mugging) is comparatively rare, but take normal precautions. Areas to be particularly careful in include Aksaray/Laleli (the city's red-light district), the Grand Bazaar

Money-Saving Tips

➜ If you plan to visit three or more museums, purchase a Museum Pass İstanbul (p140).

➜ The İstanbulkart (p137) offers a considerable discount on public-transport fares (₺1.75 as opposed to the usual ₺2, with additional transfers within a two-hour journey window ₺1).

➜ Check if your hotel offers free airport pick-ups and drop-offs.

(pickpocket central), and the streets off İstiklal Caddesi in Beyoğlu.

➡ Be careful when crossing the roads – cars are loathe to slow for pedestrians.

Telephone

Mobile Phones

➡ All visitors need to register for a SIM card, and registrations can take days to process. If you're only here for a short time, it's easiest to use international roaming.

➡ Turkey uses the standard GSM network operating on 900Mhz or 1800Mhz, so not all US and Canadian phones work here. Check with your provider before leaving home.

Phone Codes

If you're in European İstanbul and wish to call a number in Asian İstanbul, first dial ☎0, followed by ☎216. If you're in Asian İstanbul and wish to call European İstanbul, use ☎0 followed by ☎212. If you're calling a number on the same shore, there's no need to include a prefix.

Local mobile phone numbers begin with a

four-digit code starting with 05.

Country code ☎90

Intercity code
☎0 + local code

International access code ☎00

Toilets

➡ Most hotels, restaurants and museums offer Western-style toilets; public toilets and those in mosques are often of the squat variety.

Tourist Information

The Ministry of Culture & Tourism (www.turizm. gov. tr) operates four tourist information offices or booths in the city; a fifth is scheduled to open at some stage

in the future inside the Atatürk Cultural Centre on Taksim Sq in Beyoğlu. All can provide a free map of the city, but aren't very forthcoming with advice or recommendations.

Sultanahmet (Map p32, C2; ☎212-518 8754; Hippodrome, Sultanahmet; ⏰9.30am-6pm mid-Apr–Sep, 9am-5.30pm Oct–mid-Apr; 🚇Sultanahmet)

Sirkeci Train Station (Map p48, B1; ☎212-511 5888; Sirkeci Station, Ankara Caddesi, Sirkeci; ⏰9.30am-6pm mid-Apr–Sep, 9am-5.30pm Oct–mid-Apr)

Karaköy (Map p84, C7; Karaköy International Passenger Terminal, Kemankeş Caddesi, Karaköy; ⏰9.30am-5pm Mon-Sat)

Museum Pass İstanbul

Valid for 72 hours from your first museum entrance, the **Museum Pass İstanbul** (www.muze. gov.tr/museum_pass) costs ₺72 and gives entrance to Topkapı Palace and Harem, Aya Sofya, the Kariye Museum (Chora Church), the İstanbul Archaeology Museums, the Museum of Turkish & Islamic Arts and the Great Palace Mosaics Museum. Purchased individually, admission fees to these sights will cost ₺108, so the pass represents a saving of ₺36. It also allows you to bypass ticket queues. The pass can be purchased from some hotels and also from the ticket offices at Topkapı Palace, Aya Sofya, the Kariye Museum and the İstanbul Archaeology Museums.

Atatürk Airport (📞212-465 3451; International Arrivals Hall, Atatürk International Airport; 🕒9am-10pm)

Travellers with Disabilities

➡ İstanbul can be challenging for mobility-impaired travellers. Roads are potholed and pavements are often crooked and cracked.

➡ Government-run museums are free of charge for disabled visitors; many have wheelchair access.

➡ Airlines and most four- and five-star hotels have wheelchair access and at least one room set up for disabled guests.

➡ All public transport is free for the disabled; the metro and tram is wheelchair accessible.

Visas

➡ At the time of research, nationals of the following countries (among others) could enter Turkey for up to three months with only a valid passport (no visa required): Denmark, Finland, France, Germany, Greece, Italy, Israel, Japan, New Zealand, Sweden and Switzerland.

Mosque Etiquette

➡ Remove your shoes before walking on the mosque's carpet; you can leave them on shelves near the mosque door.

➡ Women should always cover their head and shoulders with a shawl or scarf; both women and men should dress modestly.

➡ Avoid visiting mosques at prayer times – within 30 minutes of when the *ezan* (call to prayer) sounds from the mosque minaret – and also around Friday lunch, when weekly sermons and group prayers are held.

➡ Speak quietly and don't use the flash on your camera if people are praying.

➡ Nationals of the following countries (among others) could enter for up to three months upon purchase of a visa sticker at their point of arrival (ie not at an embassy in advance): Australia, Canada, Ireland, Netherlands, Spain, UK and USA.

➡ Nationals of Russia and many Eastern European and Central Asian countries could enter for up to either one or two months upon purchase of a visa sticker at their point of arrival.

➡ Nationals of other countries including China and India needed to organise visas in their home countries. These were available for one-month stays.

➡ Your passport must have at least three months' validity remaining or you may not be admitted into Turkey. If you arrive at Atatürk International Airport, get your visa from the booth to the right of the Other Nationalities counter in the customs hall before you go through immigration. You can pay in pounds sterling, euros or US dollars; customs officials sometimes insist on correct change. At the time of research, Australians, Americans, Britons and most other nationalities paid €15 (US$20).

➡ See the website of the Turkish **Ministry of Foreign Affairs** (www.mfa.gov.tr) for the latest info.

Language

Pronouncing Turkish is pretty simple for English speakers as most Turkish sounds are also found in English. If you read our pronunciation guides as if they were English, you should be understood just fine. Note that the symbol **ew** represents the sound 'ee' pronounced with rounded lips (as in 'few'), and that the symbol **uh** is pronounced like the 'a' in 'ago'. The Turkish **r** is always rolled and **v** is pronounced a little softer than in English. Word stress is quite light in Turkish – in our pronunciation guides the stressed syllables are in italics.

To enhance your trip with a phrasebook, visit **lonelyplanet.com**. Lonely Planet iPhone phrasebooks are available through the Apple App store.

Basics

Hello.
Merhaba.   mer·ha·ba

Goodbye. (when leaving)
Hoşçakal.   hosh·cha·kal

Goodbye. (when staying)
Güle güle.   gew·le gew·le

Yes.
Evet.   e·vet

No.
Hayır.   ha·yuhr

Please.
Lütfen.   lewt·fen

Thank you.
Teşekkür   te·shek·kewr
ederim.   e·de·reem

Excuse me.
Bakar mısınız.   ba·kar muh·suh·nuhz

Sorry.
Özür dilerim.   er·zewr dee·le·reem

How are you?
Nasılsınız?   na·suhl·suh·nuhz

Fine, and you?
İyiyim, ya siz?   ee·yee·yeem ya seez

Do you speak English?
İngilizce   een·gee·leez·je
konuşuyor   ko·noo·shoo·yor
musunuz?   moo·soo·nooz

I don't understand.
Anlamıyorum.   an·la·muh·yo·room

Eating & Drinking

The menu, please.
Menüyü   me·new·yew
istiyorum.   ees·tee·yo·room

What would you recommend?
Ne tavsiye   ne tav·see·ye
edersiniz?   e·der·see·neez

I don't eat (meat).
(Et) yemiyorum.   (et) ye·mee·yo·room

I'd like (a/the) ...
... istiyorum.   ... ees·tee·yo·room

a (cup of) coffee
bir (fincan) kahve   beer (feen·jan) kah·ve

a (jug of) beer
bir (fıçı) bira   beer (fuh·chuh) bee·ra

Enjoy your meal.
Afiyet olsun.   a·fee·yet ol·soon

Cheers!
Şerefe!   she·re·fe

That was delicious!
Nefisti!   ne·fees·tee

The bill, please.
Hesap lütfen.   he·sap lewt·fen

Shopping

I'd like to buy ...
... almak   al·mak
istiyorum.   ees·tee·yo·room

I'm just looking.
Sadece   sa·de·je
bakıyorum.   ba·kuh·yo·room

How much is it?
Ne kadar?   ne ka·dar

It's too expensive.
Bu çok pahalı.   boo chok pa·ha·luh

Do you have something cheaper?
Daha ucuz   da·ha oo·jooz
birşey var mı?   beer·shay var muh

Emergencies

Help!
İmdat!   eem·dat

Call a doctor!
Doktor çağırın!   dok·tor cha·uh·ruhn

Call the police!
Polis çağırın!   po·lees cha·uh·ruhn

I'm lost.
Kayboldum.   kai·bol·doom

I'm ill.
Hastayım.   has·ta·yuhm

Where's the toilet?
Tuvalet nerede?   too·va·let ne·re·de

Time & Numbers

What time is it?
Saat kaç?   sa·at kach

It's (10) o'clock.
Saat (on).   sa·at (on)

in the morning
öğleden evvel   er·le·den ev·vel

in the afternoon
öğleden sonra   er·le·den son·ra

in the evening
akşam   ak·sham

now
şimdi   sheem·dee

yesterday	*dün*	dewn
today	*bugün*	boo·gewn
tomorrow	*yarın*	ya·ruhn
1	*bir*	beer
2	*iki*	ee·kee
3	*üç*	ewch
4	*dört*	dert
5	*beş*	besh
6	*altı*	al·tuh
7	*yedi*	ye·dee
8	*sekiz*	se·keez
9	*dokuz*	do·kooz
10	*on*	on

Transport & Directions

Where is the (market)?
(Pazar yeri)   (pa·zar ye·ree)
nerede?   ne·re·de

What's the address?
Adresi nedir?   ad·re·see ne·deer

Can you show me (on the map)?
Bana (haritada)   ba·na (ha·ree·ta·da)
gösterebilir   gers·te·re·bee·leer
misin?   mee·seen

Please put the meter on.
Lütfen   lewt·fen
taksimetreyi   tak·see·met·re·yee
çalıştırın.   cha·luhsh·tuh·ruhn

I'd like a ticket to ...
... bir bilet   ... beer bee·let
lütfen.   lewt·fen

Does it stop at ...?
... durur mu?   ... doo·roor moo

I'd like to get off at ...
... inmek   ... een·mek
istiyorum.   ees·tee·yo·room

Behind the Scenes

Send Us Your Feedback

We love to hear from travellers – your comments help make our books better. We read every word, and we guarantee that your feedback goes straight to the authors. Visit **lonelyplanet.com/contact** to submit your updates and suggestions.

Note: We may edit, reproduce and incorporate your comments in Lonely Planet products such as guidebooks, websites and digital products, so let us know if you don't want your comments reproduced or your name acknowledged. For a copy of our privacy policy visit lonelyplanet.com/privacy.

Our Readers

Thanks to the travellers who used the last edition and wrote to us with helpful hints, useful advice and interesting anecdotes:

Simin Atayman, Ian Dunsford, Hamilton Hay, Ilse Hogendorf, Nicholas Lunn, Susan Manly

Sabancı Çetindoğan, Ercan Tanrıvermiş, Ann Nevans, Tina Nevans, Jennifer Gaudet, Özlem Tuna, Shellie Corman, Mehmet Umur, Emel Güntaş, Tuna Mersinli, Halûk Dursun, İnci Döndaş, İlber Ortayli, Selin Rozanes, Ansel Mullins, Megan Clark, Atilla Tuna and Elif Aytekin.

Virginia's Thanks

Many thanks to Pat Yale, Faruk Boyacı, Tahir Karabaş, Eveline Zoutendijk, George Grundy, Saffet Tonguç, Demet

Acknowledgments

Cover photograph: Ortaköy Mosque and the Bosphorus Bridge, İstanbul, Turkey, Michele Falzone/AWL

This Book

This 4th edition of Lonely Planet's Pocket *İstanbul* guide was researched and written by Virginia Maxwell, who also wrote the previous two editions. This guidebook was commissioned in Lonely Planet's London office, and produced by the following:

Commissioning Editor Clifton Wilkinson **Coord-** inating Editors Susan Paterson, Gabrielle Stefanos **Coordinating Cartographer** Rachel Imeson **Coordinating Layout Designer** Jacqui Saunders **Managing Editor** Brigitte Ellemor **Senior Editor** Catherine Naghten **Managing Cartographers** Anita Banh, Adrian Persoglia **Managing Layout Designer** Jane Hart **Assisting Cartographer** Jeff Cameron **Cover** **Research** Naomi Parker **Internal Image Research** Aude Vauconsant **Language Content** Branislava Vladisavljevic **Thanks to** Shahara Ahmed, Dan Austin, Imogen Bannister, Lauren Egan, Ryan Evans, Tobias Gattineau, Jouve India, Asha Ioculari, Annelies Mertens, Trent Paton, Raphael Richards, Averil Robertson, Fiona Siseman, Gerard Walker

Index

See also separate subindexes for:

🍴 **Eating p149**

🍷 **Drinking p150**

🎭 **Entertainment p150**

🛍 **Shopping p151**

Sights p000
Map Pages **p000**

🍽 Eating

Our Writer

Virginia Maxwell

Although based in Australia, Virginia spends much of her year researching guidebooks in the Mediterranean countries. Of these, Turkey is unquestionably her favourite. As well as working on the previous two editions of *Pocket İstanbul*, she is also the author of Lonely Planet's *İstanbul* city guide and the İstanbul chapter of Lonely Planet's *Turkey* guide, and she writes about the city for a host of international magazines and websites. Virginia usually travels with partner Peter and son Max, who have grown to love Turkey as much as she does. Read more about Virginia at lonelyplanet.com/members/virginiamaxwell.

Published by Lonely Planet Publications Pty Ltd
ABN 36 005 607 983
4th edition – Feb 2013
ISBN 978 1 74220 038 5
© Lonely Planet 2013 Photographs © as indicated 2013
10 9 8 7 6 5 4
Printed in China